ZOMBIE
SCHOOL
CONFIDENTIAL

ALSO BY SEAN HOADE

ZOMBIE SCHOOL CONFIDENTIAL

by Sean Hoade
("Professor Zombie")
&
Matt Scalici
of FilmNerds.com

A FilmNerds® Book

Cover Art by Putnam Finch

Special Thanks to Shari Nickles and Ann Hoade

Foreword

As someone with an obsessive, completionist mind, it has never been enough to simply like something. If I find something I like, I dive into it, surround myself with it, absorbing as much knowledge and discussion as I can on the topic.

I started FilmNerds.com in 2009 with a group of like-minded friends as an attempt to satisfy this desire to take a more intense and focused approach to discussing the films, directors, actors, and genres I had spent so much time obsessing over. We all attended the University of Alabama, where we spent time arguing over movies in the student newspaper as critics, on campus radio, and even eventually in our own student organization.

While we've gone on to create all kinds of fun projects at FilmNerds.com in the years since its founding, from our Shelf of Shame series in which we force ourselves to watch notable films we shamefully haven't seen yet, to my Back to the Movies series in which I watched and reviewed the fifty highest grossing films from 1983. But podcasts have always been the heart of FilmNerds.com, thanks in large part to the special chemistry and group dynamic that can only come from many years of arguing with and mercilessly mocking each other.

When the site was founded, podcasts were still in the early years of their growing popularity and became interested in the idea of creating a multipart series of podcasts that would allow my partners and me to more fully explore a topic. In two of our early podcast "miniseries" attempts, we analyzed the complete feature-length works of Charlie Chaplin and in another looked at all of Woody Allen's black-and-white films. These kinds of multipart explorations of a given topic fed my insatiable nerd hunger and I began looking outside my close group of friends for a collaborator that could help me take the podcasts to the next level.

That's where Sean Hoade comes into the picture.

Sean taught several of my FilmNerds friends during his time in the English department at Alabama and was recommended to me as a potential guest of interest for the podcast. When I approached Sean with my idea to explore the genre, it was with a combination of excitement and intimidation. Sean was exactly the kind of voice I wanted to bring into the fold for our podcasts but his knowledge base on the topic I wanted to explore with him, zombies, was not exactly an area of expertise for me. Once Sean agreed to record the podcasts with me, I set out on an epic binge-watching session of zombie films, from mainstream classics (some of which I shamefully hadn't seen yet) to obscure, foreign takes on the genre.

Several weeks and numerous nightmares later, Sean and I finally recorded our series and the finished product exceeded even my wildest expectations. Throughout the seven installments of our series, we explored the zombie genre on film from its technical and cinematic conventions to function as a form of gory social commentary and so much more.

Being a moderator and interviewer in these discussions didn't just give me a great series of podcasts I felt proud to publish on myself. They also helped change my opinions about the value of great zombie stories and what they can tell us about the society we live in today. I hope you get as much out of reading our discussions as I got from participating in them.

Matt Scalici
FilmNerds.com

Table of Contents

Introduction

One way you can tell that the zombie craze is nowhere near over is that, in the five years or so since these interviews were broadcast, a dozen movies about the living dead, several zombie television shows (including the massively popular *The Walking Dead*), and scads and scads of zombie fiction have cropped up to be enthusiastically devoured by viewers, readers, and thinkers. Any book trying to be comprehensive about the latest zombie entertainment would be outdated as soon as it hit stores.

That's why I'm glad that Matt Scalici and I took a different tack for *Zombie School Confidential*. In the pages that follow, you will find that we deal with the underlying themes of any zombie story—fears of alienation, bodily corruption, metaphysical loss of self, and much more. We show you the history of the zombie mythos, from its inception in Haiti to the epoch-making films of George Romero to the more-intimate zombie movies like *Fido* and *Zombie Honeymoon*.

Readers will find this in-depth discussion of every aspect of zombies in our culture a valuable tool when watching or reading about the undead. You will understand why zombie entertainment speaks to us even after 80-something years. It is always new, it is always growing, and it is always hungry for our brains—but this time to fill them.

After the seven interviews, included for your reading pleasure is a "clip file" of other articles including interviews with me about zombie culture as well as an essay I wrote for *The Sun* on the occasion of the release of the movie version of Max Brooks' *World War Z.*

I taught one of the very first for-credit university classes about zombies, and my iTunes interviews with Matt receive about 90,000 downloads every year. In this book is the fruit of my experience as "Professor Zombie," Matt's in-depth knowledge of film, and everything you need to become a zombie expert yourself and wow your friends at the coffee shop or bar after having seen the latest undead epic production.

The field of "zombie studies," if you will, is exploding even as I write these words in 2015. But what you hold in your hands (or are reading on a screen) is the prerequisite for any serious investigation of what—and how—zombies mean to us.

Enjoy! And remember: never, *ever* leave your safe place in a zombocalypse to save someone you think may still be alive "out there." It makes for heroics in the movies, but in real life, it just provides a little more meat for and a new member of the zombie hordes.

Sean Hoade
Las Vegas, Nevada

Lesson 1
An Introduction to Zombies

Matt Scalici, *FilmNerds.com*: We are beginning a new podcast series here today, and the topic will be the ever-interesting subject of zombies in film. With us for this series is, I have to say, by far the most qualified guest we have ever had on FilmNerds.com. He is an instructor of English at the University of Alabama, where he has taught several fascinating "Special Topics In Literature classes—on superheroes, on the Apocalypse, and most relevant to us, one on the subject of zombies, a class which has received international attention. Sean Hoade is our guest expert for this series. Welcome to the podcast, Sean.

Sean Hoade, Writer and "Professor Zombie": Thank you. The only thing I love more than zombies is movies about zombies.

FN: I always like to give myself a little refresher course before we do podcasts, so I've been in a particularly demented state of mind this week just with the research I've been doing, so it's been interesting.

Well, during this series we are going to delve deep into this genre of film, this very interesting and complex and always-evolving genre, and, rather than go film-by-film as we've done in some of our other FilmNerd series, this time we're going to take a look at different aspects of the entire genre, the different sorts of conventions and areas of interest within the zombie genre. First, we're going to present a little introduction to the zombie genre. We're going to look at how it came about as well as why we're doing this series: Exploring why the zombie genre has become such a big deal in American—indeed, global—film.

So Sean, how far back does the zombie film go? Obviously, zombies have been an idea that has been a part of various cultures and civilizations for a long time, but as far as appearing in the medium of film, how far back does this go?

Hoade: Actually, let me clarify something first. Most people think that the zombie concept as we understand it started a lot earlier than it actually does because the idea of other famous movie monsters like vampires or werewolves goes back a thousand years or more, and even Shelley's *Frankenstein* is almost 200 years ago, for instance.

Vampires and lychanthropes were known and feared at least back to the Middle Ages, possibly earlier, and mummies obviously go back to Ancient Egypt, but the zombie is actually almost entirely a cinematic creation, so it's really appropriate to do this FilmNerds movie podcast because zombies as we define them now didn't exist before movies, and in fact, the concept of zombies in the West didn't exist at all until maybe four years prior to the first zombie movie. I would say the zombie idea in the West was launched with the 1928 book by William Seabrook called *The Magic Island,* which is about Haiti. To this day, Haiti is where people think of something existing that is extremely close to "real" zombies.

We always think of Haiti because of the Seabrook book and the scientific investigations made by Harvard ethnobotanist Wade Davis decades later. Many people know that in Haiti, they allegedly use the powerful venom of the puffer fish to put people into a state that seems zombie-like. Those zombies aren't like the Romero zombies or the ones that eat your brain or whatever, but they are what we think of when we think of what could possibly be a *real* zombie.

With the publication of *The Magic Island,* Haiti mania and zombie mania took over in the United States. People were crazy about the idea, and there was a play in 1932 based on a chapter of the book called *Zombie* that was popular and people went to see it. At that time it was considered quite scary, and filmmakers ran with it and made a movie *very* similar to the stage play called *White Zombie* in that same year, 1932. What happened is they basically stole the entire plot and idea from the play *Zombie,* but in perfect Hollywood style, they said, "We don't have to pay for this because the story is based on a nonfiction book, based on things that allegedly happened," so they got away with stealing from the people who made the play, who of course stole Seabrook's ideas in the first place. What could be more Hollywood than that? And it was an immediate smash success on film. It made $8 million, a huge amount for the time.

FN: We've seen that with other subgenres of horror from that era as well. Obviously, the whole Dracula/vampire film was started with *Nosferatu,* which is just a cinematic ripoff of *Dracula.* [**Note:** The producers of the 1922 *Nosferatu* were sued by the Stoker estate for copyright infringement, and every copy of the film was collected and burned ... except one that was found years later and is the basis for every recording of the film we have today.]

Hoade: Right, right, and of course, *White Zombie* wasn't exactly a ripoff of Dracula, but then you had Bela Lugosi in it as the zombie master. It definitely traded on his image as the dark and mysterious stranger, coming right off of his success as Dracula. Sadly, when he was negotiating to make the movie—and the *White* Zombie producers really wanted him because of the popularity of Dracula, which came out in 1931—he tipped his hand that he really needed money, so again, in perfect Hollywood style, they screwed him, and they ended up paying him just $800 for this movie that made $8 million.

Obviously this is a history long before the Romero films, but *White Zombie* is the one movie everyone looks at as really starting this entire genre. However, what made the zombie what we think of today would be *Night of the Living Dead*, the first zombie film from George Romero.

FN: What are some of the conventions and the stereotypical zombie elements that we see in all zombie movies today? What were some of those that Romero created that weren't really part of that genre before *Night of the Living Dead?*

Hoade: It's really interesting. I'll take you through a little bit of history: In *White Zombie,* the idea is that there is black magic of one kind or another, and that idea was taken from *The Magic Island,* a book which purported to document actual V*odoun* practices that were going on in Haiti. The title of the film being *White Zombie* changes the horror concept from slave masters in Haiti with black zombies to, "Oh no, these are white zombies! The Negro necromancers are taking over our white women!"and things like that, the usual paranoia, the racist paranoia of the time, so we had that. Extremely exploitative and racist, and extraordinarily successful.

As these race-baiting zombie movies—the Asian undead were also popular monsters fighting the American military for years—fell in quality and then in number throughout the '30s and '40s, you got away from the idea of the zombie master and the Haitian zombie in general. In the 1950s, when everyone was worried about nuclear attack, with nuclear fallout changing our genetics and making us something *other*, they made *The Zombies of Mora Tau*, which was a war movie, and this obscure film introduced the idea of the contagious zombie. Romero didn't actually come up with that one. In the Romero films, if you're a zombie and you bite someone or otherwise infect them, they die and rise again as a zombie. Romero had that to work with because of *Zombies of Mora Tau*.

FN: How is the zombiism spread in that film? I'm assuming they are not yet the man-eating variety of zombie.

Hoade: It was a little unclear. If the zombie attacks you and kills you, if you're killed by a zombie—it's almost like being a werewolf, except a werewolf was actually alive, and you become a living werewolf yourself. [Note: The concept of a bite from a werewolf turning a victim into a werewolf comes from the 1941 Universal movie *The Wolf Man*, starring Lon Chaney, Jr. In that same film, the idea of silver killing werewolves was also introduced.]

It's the same thing here in *Mora Tau*: If you're attacked and killed by a zombie, then you become a zombie as well. They didn't have the same ideas of virology as we have now. I mean, when you see zombie movies or really many different kinds of monster movies or horror movies now, you see that they take into account our knowledge and fears of viral infection, but they didn't really have that in the '50s yet. They didn't really understand viral contagion the way that we understand it now, but they definitely understood idea of radioactive contamination.

The movie was a little unclear on how exactly the transfer happened, but it wasn't black magic, and that was a really big change in the concept. Now it was something naturalistic and not based on race baiting. Then the genius of Romero was that he took the lemons of losing the scary zombie master and he made lemonade—he asked himself, "Okay, well, what's scary? The living dead are scary." So they're going to make a movie about the living dead, but they're making this for $119,000, I think, which was nothing for a 35mm movie. They had to shoot it in black and white, though. And they were making this movie with friends, staying in the farmhouse where they filmed it, smoking reefer, having a good time, and they put their heads together: "How can we really make this zombie movie *something* big"—they didn't call them "zombies" in the movie, of course—but "this living dead movie, how can we make it something that's really going to get attention? What's the most offensive thing that we can get away with?"

Then they hit right on it: cannibalism. Cannibalism is the biggest cultural taboo next to incest, and nobody really wants to watch that kind of thing in a movie. Incest is something some people did, taboo or not; it was too *real* to be fun-scary. But nobody's actually *eating* other people, right? The idea that these living dead will eat you and then what's left of you will get up and start eating other people was the most disgusting, horrifying, attention-grabbing thing that Romero and his associates could think of. So they put it in there, and of course it worked perfectly. It worked *beautifully*. It scared the *shit* out of audiences. It's like, We have these living dead. Not only are they risen from the grave, maybe because of some radiation from a crashed satellite but it doesn't matter—they want to *eat your flesh* and make *you* do the same thing to others.

It doesn't matter how this has all happened—you're just trying to survive! There were a million "people trapped while monsters try to get at them" movies at the drive-ins and even in some bigger-budget productions like the Hammer horror films. But Romero & Co. added the flesh-eating part, and that completely disgusted everyone to the point where they couldn't look away. It was so transgressive, some viewers watched simply out of horrified awe at the audacity of *Night of the Living Dead*.

This naturally inspired—because good ideas get exploited immediately—all of the Italian gross-out movies of the late '6os and early '7os with the living dead, really just excuses for extended scenes of the most disgusting violence and cannibalism, and Italian audiences loved it. Some of these Argento films and a few others have survived to become kind of offbeat classics in America. But it was Romero put the two ideas together of the contagion and the cannibalism to come up with something unique, and he just, with his subsequent movies, especially *Dawn of the Dead* in '78, just took it to its Omega.

He introduced the idea of the cannibalistic zombie, and now when you think of zombies, what do you think? They're going to eat you, right? They're going to kill you, eat you, and then you're going to get up and eat people, which you *really* don't want to happen to you.

FN: Like you said, that is the defining trait of zombie movies today that really came out of *Night,* but one of the other things, just to touch on briefly, that Romero is credited with introducing into the genre is making it about a little more than just the surface terror, that he injected some interesting subtext into what were still essentially monster movies. In the later installments of this podcast series, we will touch on some of those various subtexts, but just to stay on this very surface level that we're talking about right now, some of these conventions we talk about that Romero helped define and codify have been defied and played with a little bit as we've gone on in subsequent decades.

But some ideas are getting tweaked, "de-codified," if you will. We have zombies that are fast and athletic, making them more dangerous than ever before. We saw that in Danny Boyle's *28 Days Later...* and its sequel and also in the remake of *Dawn of the Dead*, which really even irked a few more people because you have the whole Romero convention of the lumbering zombie being thrown out the window in a remake of a Romero movie.

What do you think about playing with that zombie formula. Are there any examples where it worked for you, or are you pretty much across the board against messing with the Romero zombie conventions?

Hoade: Well, the great thing about a convention is as soon as it becomes the convention, it becomes a sandbox for creative people. As soon as you have a convention, it is time to subvert that convention. I think that the "zoombies," the fast zombies—

FN: Zoombies, nice.

Hoade: [Laughs.] Yes, I call them *zoombies*. I have to tell you, 2004's *Dawn of the Dead* scared the living hell out of me, and *28 Days Later...*, same thing. If you think of that same year's zoom-rom-com *Shaun of the Dead*, you've still got the lumbering zombies, but they're kind of amusing and played for a little bit of laughs in the beginning. Amusing, of course, until they rip your throat out.

But they're kind of funny, since they're off-balance and lumbering. There is nothing funny about a running zombie. It is just pure terror.

FN: That's what makes, like we mentioned, *28 Days Later*... and the 2004 *Dawn of the Dead*, I mean, they're so different from when you watch something like *Day of the Dead* or the original *Dawn of the Dead*, where there are no moments of levity at all. I mean, these are intense, just, you know, gritty thrillers all the way through. There is *no* break in those movies.

Hoade: Right! This is not your father's zombie movie. This isn't one where you can go, "Oh! I'm so scared! Look at the mummy coming after me and I can briskly walk away" or whatever. This is something where, if you are not completely on your toes, and maybe even if you are, you are doomed. They will run after you at superhuman speeds, and you know, I think as far as—I mean, it's kind of funny to talk about realism in a zombie movie, talking about reanimated dead people coming after you, but let's say that we accept that—in terms of "I'm going to scare your pants off," it makes perfect sense and is wholly effective. Also, Danny Boyle's *28 Days Later...*, as I'm sure your listeners know, is not *technically* a zombie movie. They infected are not actually dead. They've got a virus and so become cannibalistic and extremely contagious—in fact, people wouldn't even think of that as a zombie movie if they weren't.

So even though a purist would say it's not actually a zombie movie, I think it's operating on the same basic fears as a "true" undead zombie movie: like you mentioned, the contagion and the fact that these monsters are in the form of humans, which is a very important element of the zombie genre, and that you could easily become one of them and do horrible things that repel you as long as you're uninfected.

Hoade: Yes, that's actually also in *28 Days Later...*—that's how it becomes a zombie movie, and I do think it is a zombie movie. Another way is that, as they say in the original *night of the Living Dead*, your mother is *not* your mother anymore. If she gets infected with the Rage Virus, she is only someone who wants to infect you with the Rage Virus. It doesn't matter if she's technically alive or dead.

FN: This is exploited quite well in *Shaun of the Dead,* and I'm sure we'll talk about that later in the series.

Hoade: Right. *Shaun of the Dead* is great at subverting a lot of those conventions, which is why it's funny, but one of the many things I love about *Shaun of the Dead* is that it's also scary.

FN: Absolutely. It works as a horror film. If you watch some of Simon Pegg and Nick Frost's other work, *Hot Fuzz* and their brilliant British television series, *Spaced*, I mean, those guys are very funny, but it feels less like parody or even homage, and more like a sincerely great version riffing on whatever they're working from.

Hoade: I think they're complete geniuses, but Romero, he brought something else into the zombie world. He made these zombie movies not just about these creatures that want to kill you and eat you and turn you into zombies. Accidentally is *Night* and thereafter very intentionally, he made the zombie movie a platform where we can have a serious discussion about society—this is the subtext that we're going to talk about later.

He said, "You know, we can talk about in *Night of the Living Dead*, we can talk about racism. If we're talking about *Dawn of the Dead*, we can talk about American consumerism. If we're talking about *Day of the Dead*, we can talk about the military industrial complex, right? If we're talking about *Land of the Dead*, we can talk about the gated communities and separation of rich and poor in America in a way that's never been done before," and if we're looking at *Diary of the Dead*, his latest and probably final entry in it [Note: By publication time, Romero had directed one more entry in the series, 2010's *Survival of the Dead*], we're talking about the YouTube generation. You know, I heard about a motocross racer who had just gotten killed at a public exhibition—his motorcycle crashed and he hit his head and was killed. As soon as I heard about that, I went on YouTube and was able to find footage of it. Multiply that times 3 billion and you would have Internet coverage of the zombie apocalypse.

Everybody's filming everything all the time, and because of the Internet we have all these ways to instantly share that information, and that's what *Diary of the Dead* gives us—yes, it's a scary zombie movie and I think it's extremely effective, but it's also about the YouTube generation. Some people hate it because it goes back to the initial zombie infestation, but I think it was a fresher entry than was *Land of the Dead*.

So that's something that Romero really started. Romero made legitimate the idea of "This isn't just a monster movie—this is socially as well as culturally relevant."

FN: Yes, absolutely, and that's why the zombie subgenre is worth dedicating a whole podcast series to, and we'll be looking at these various different ways that the zombie genre has been used to take a look at certain aspects of our society and of what it means to be human.

Hoade: This is just a foundational thing, so I think it should be in this first podcast: Zombies are actually the ultimate movie creature because they don't think—they only *do*. They only do, and that's something that can be captured on film better than any other medium like novels or graphic novels or, you know, radio shows or whatever. Really, a movie is the perfect place to have the zombie menace, and so it's especially appropriate that you're devoting a film podcast to this.

FN: Because it's all action. There's no need for inner monologue or further explanation. What you see is what's happening with a zombie.

Hoade: Right. No zombie has ever asked, What's my motivation? There's no plotting or scheming, there's no negotiating or surrendering, there's nothing but searching and killing and eating and making more undead.

FN: In our second episode of this series, we're going to be talking about the very idea that Sean just mentioned: how race relations are examined in some famous zombie films that on the surface just seem to be about the living dead.

Lesson 2
The Living As Minority

Matt Scalici, *FilmNerds.com*: Today we're going to look at the issue of race as it's dealt with in some various zombie films. First off, Sean, George Romero is really the guy I think that gets mentioned the most often as being the guy that first made the connection between racial issues and zombies on film. What were some of the ways that Romero approached racial issues in his zombie films? And you can take us through *Night of the Living Dead* and *Dawn of the Dead, Day of the Dead,* any of his films really, have touched on this, but take us through what you think Romero had to say on this topic.

Sean Hoade, Writer and "Professor Zombie": It's funny because with a lot of things that happen with classics, this was another example of something that was accidental. Not that Romero isn't, you know, awake to race topics and things like that, but actually, when they were making the original *Night of the Living Dead,* they said, "Well, who among our friends"—because Romero and his friends made commercials and they did TV spots and things like that, so they knew people who were actors or wanted to be actors, and they said—"is the best actor? We need that person to play Ben." This was the lead in *Night of the Living Dead,* and they said, "Our friend Duane Jones is the best actor!" He happened to be black and so, okay, well, Ben, the lead character of the *Night of the Living Dead* is black, okay, great, done. That's how we ended up with the protagonist of *Night of the Living Dead* being a black person in 1968, which is not exactly a time when you would expect to see that in a movie that isn't, you know, *Guess Who's Coming to Dinner?* or some other movie that's explicitly about race.

So what he did with that, with this stroke of accidental genius, is he made it about race *without* making it about race. He said you have to accept that this person, Ben, is the most with-it person out of all the characters in the movie. He's the one who actually comes up with the way to protect them from the zombies—or the ghouls, as they call them in that movie—or scare them off. He's the one that comes up with the idea to to fill the truck with gas so they can get away (which doesn't work out, but that wasn't his fault). He does it all, and he's this competent, very middle-class black man. I mean, he's wearing a cardigan sweater through most of the movie. He's sort of the nonthreatening black man.

Hoade: And no one ever in the entire movie makes any comment about his race. You have the Coopers, you have Harry Cooper. He and Ben face off during the whole movie. Harry is going to shoot Ben and doesn't, and Ben actually shoots him and kills him, but Harry doesn't call him anything bad—there are no racial epithets used, and that's because when they wrote the part, when they wrote the movie, it wasn't written for, you know, "a black person." It was just written as a character, and they stayed with the script. They had to stay with the script because they weren't doing any improv because their film stock was limited. So they stuck to the script, and the script didn't have any comments about race because it wasn't about that. So it ended up being this watershed movie where viewers have to accept that the most competent, calmest, most with-it person is a black person— which goes against many of the stereotypes of the day—and it all worked quite well. I think that's part of what made the movie's reputation among the critics and intelligentsia, the people whose opinions mattered.

FN: Had the part of Ben been cast with a white actor, race wouldn't have been an issue in the reception and discussion of the film, because there is no explicit commentary on race. It's all just perception borne out of the context that that film was released in.

Hoade: Exactly. There's absolutely no explicit mention of race whatsoever. There is, however— if you look at it, once Duane Jones is cast and once they make the movie, you can start looking at the movie in this way that says, "Oh, wow, this has a lot to do with race." This is one of the great things about the zombie movie genre in general, but especially *Night of the Living Dead*, is that you have a core group of people who are alive, and if most of the people in the world (or in *Night*, at least the general area) becomes zombies, then the actual living are kind of an elite, aren't they? And this elite is allegorical to the white elite at that time. We didn't have a black president back then, you know? Martin Luther King had just been murdered. So you've got this group of people being surrounded by a group who *used* to be a minority, but due to its overwhelming and prolific procreation has now taken over and is threatening everything that is valuable to you, including your life. This is the way that a lot of white people—a lot of white people now but especially back then—thought of black people as a whole.

FN: So the film inadvertently ends up preying on this deep-seated fear in that group that you mentioned, that basically they were going to be swallowed by this group that they viewed as scum, just *less* than them, not just displacing their cultural values (and wealth, and hegemony) rather than literally changing them into members of the sub group.

Hoade: Exactly. One of the things that is so horrifying about these apocalyptic type of movies—I mean, it's *fascinating* but it's horrifying—is that it's not only that most people are going to die, if not everybody, but that civilization is going to fall, civilization as we understand it is going to fall because of the sheer proliferation of the once-minority group.

Also, tellingly, zombies can do things that we can't do, you know? In a lot of stories, they're stronger, they have greater stamina, they don't need rest or to use the bathroom, and of course they can bite you and turn you into one of them. An analogue might be the racist fathers not wanting their daughters to date or marry black men, because the children would then be a part of the "other" that the racists were frightened of in the first place.

This all spoke to 1968 America. If you're surrounded by these people and they're challenging your way of life, you fight back as hard as you can, but both whites and blacks who saw this movie picked up on allegorical themes in something Romero didn't even intend as racial commentary. People say, "Oh, look, there are these zombies or ghouls that live a different lifestyle than we do," and that's putting it mildly, isn't it? Eating people's guts and all this stuff.

I mean, what fiction does, right, it tells the truth, but as Emily Dickinson said, it "tells it slant" and so it exaggerates, but fictional monsters are showing what real-life viewers think of those who live differently, who are different from themselves—and they are directly threatening "us." It's just been very powerful.

FN: Then, ten years later we get *Dawn of the Dead*, which was Romero's second big zombie release, widely viewed by a lot of people as the movie that, even more than *Night of the Living Dead*, made this genre take off.

Hoade: A masterpiece.

FN: There's some—as we said, there's no explicit mention of race in *Night of the Living Dead*. At the very beginning of *Dawn of the Dead*, we see some very explicit dealings with racial matters. Talk about *Dawn of the Dead*'s approach to race.

Hoade: Romero didn't know the golden product he had when he made *Night of the Living Dead*. He said, "We're making a horror movie, it's going to be fun, we'll make our money back I hope, maybe some more." Of course, it became a huge, international hit, very influential. When he was making *Dawn of the Dead*, he realized that he had a platform, an entertainment bully pulpit, and he really played that up in an appropriate way. The movie starts off in the projects for people on welfare and things, and they have been—because of their religious beliefs, they don't want to just throw Grandma into the fire or chop her head off—they've been just tying up the zombies and putting them in the basement. So the cops—the SWAT teams and stuff—come, and they're going get the people out to save them, and also kill the zombies again. But from the very beginning, you've got a white cop talking about N-word this and "spics" and all this stuff and how dirty they are and how bad ... but not anything negative (or positive) about the zombies at all.

I mean, this cop spouts how "they" really disgust him, and he goes on this killing spree, you know? He can shoot anyone and say, "I thought that was a zombie, and that's why he had to be taken out." Again, though, he is expressing what a lot of people in the '70s, whether they would admit it or not, thought: "*We* are paying for these people to live here, *we the taxpayers* are paying for these people on welfare, and that's not right, and if we have a chance, we should get rid of them." This is as if no black or Hispanic people paid taxes! I mean, nobody would come out and say that, except maybe somebody with the Ku Klux Klan or something—but that is what I think Romero was trying to tap into there, so he made it totally explicit. I think very consciously, Romero cast the fabulous black actor Ken Foree to play the male protagonist, once again the one who really keeps it together—

FN: Just like in *Night of the Living Dead*.

Hoade: Right, but this time he did it consciously, and Foree's character is named Peter, and if you have a black man named Peter, you've immediately got that "black men have big peters" idea at the forefront, which is a major element of the white man's fear that better-endowed black men will take the white women away. Then you've got Peter's white friend, Roger—they're white and black, but they don't comment on the difference there. It's just we're on the same side—the living—we're friends, and we will fight the zombies together. They do make comments about how much taller Peter is than Roger, and some of the best dialogue in the movie—and actually was improvised—is when they're joking on the radio when they're moving the trucks to block the mall, about how Ken's this giant and Scott is this midget, but it has nothing to do with race, even though Romero has put the races are together very purposefully. Of course, at the end of *Dawn of the Dead*, you've got Peter, a black man, and Francine, played by Gaylen Ross, a pregnant white woman. They're the survivors, and they're the ones who fly off to, at best, an uncertain future, but they escape *together*. Now, the baby that she would have, since the father was Flyboy, will be white, not of mixed race, but I think the point is made that they would be the new Adam and Eve, a black man and a white woman, which even in '78, after over a decade of civil rights protests and race riots, was still a jarring idea to middle America. But Romero did all that very intentionally and very, very well in terms of making people uncomfortable within a movie where we are *horribly* uncomfortable in a fun way, because zombies and motorcycle gangs and such.

In *Dawn,* he's more intentionally pushing the envelope. Brilliantly, he's *not* doing this typically preachy idea of "Look how absurd it is that the races can't get along!" It's more of holding up a mirror to the audience and letting them see if the image is in fact theirs.

Let's say there's a zombie infestation or takeover or whatever you want to call it. Who are you more like? Are you more like another living human who happens to be a different race, or are you more like the *undead monster* that wants to eat your guts? Of course, I would say that you're more like the living person, and I would hope that's what people would choose. But racism runs deep indeed, so who knows? Maybe someone would rather be undead than be a black hero and survivor.

Either way, the race allegories here just work really well again as they did in *Night,* and even though he was more explicit in this one, it's not to the point of overkill or redundancy. Romero uses great skill in making it so there's never anything said about race between the two men, between Peter and Roger, "Hey, I'm black! Hey you're white! And we're getting along, isn't this swell! Here we are, we're surviving, ebony and ivory!"

FN: And in the next film in the series, *Day of the Dead*, we have yet another heroic, got-it-together black man, who once again is one of the voices of reason and indeed ends up once again with the white female protagonist of the film.

Hoade: Yes! Once again, you have the black actor, Terry Alexander, who is playing a Jamaican, you know, but is essentially American. You having him playing John, who is, as you said, one of the main voices of reason in the film. You've also got Jarlath Conroy playing the Irishman who is always Jesus, Joseph, and Mary-ing every five minutes and drinking from a flask of whiskey. So obviously, Romero wasn't against *all* stereotypes. [Laughs.]

At the end of *Day of the Dead* the Jamaican and the Irishman escape with Sarah to the island spot to live out the rest of their lives and maybe reproduce, maybe not. Regardless, you've got the black man again being really the voice of reason, and that means a lot in a talky movie. There's a *lot* of talking going on, and in fact this may be the most philosophicalof the entire Romero *Dead* series. They didn't have the budget for much else. They originally had a $7 million budget, and studio wanted it to be an R-rated film.

FN: As opposed to not being releasable because of theaters' policies against X-rated or unrated movies.

Hoade: Just so. Being X-rated at that time didn't mean it was pornographic—*Midnight Cowboy* was rated X and won Best Picture—but it was the equivalent of what is now NC-17, much less marketable. But, God love him, Romero stuck to his vision. He said, well, all right, I'll let you chop off half the budget, but I'm going to make the movie that I want to make. And it's funny because you look at the gore effects from back then and, even though they're well done, are extremely fake-looking compared with special effects now. You watch it now and you're like "They wanted to give *that* an X rating for gore? But, you know, it was 1985, a different world for independent filmmakers like Romero.

Anyway, you've got Terry Alexander as John, the Jamaican man, who is the one who speaks truth to power, really. He talks to Captain Rhodes—played by Joe Pilato in the kind of role big stars would fight for. Anyway, John stands up and talks to Captain Rhodes in a way that Sarah can't, in a way that Rhodes' own men— the sergeant and privates who are under him— can't, because John is the only one who can fly the helicopter. He is the black man, and they do make comments on that. Captain Rhodes calls him a "jungle bunny." There's a little out-and-out racism among the military men there, setting up even more tension in a situation already tense from cramped spaces, science vs. mere survival, and of course the thousands of zombies at the fences trying to get in to the compound.

And there's serious—even threatening—sexism, too. The soldiers are always saying really sexually crude remarks to Sarah, the female lead who is a scientist, and she's got nowhere to go if they want to rape her or otherwise abuse her sexually. Nothing really comes of that, but it is always a tension bubbling right beneath the surface.

But anyway, it's not like race isn't noticed in this case, but John defeats it by being the only one who has the skill to get them out of there, so they have to respect that even if they don't respect his race, which apparently they don't. He is the only one who can save any of them if they need to abandon their facility.

FN: Yes, and I want to take a look at—you know, we've mentioned in all three of these cases that we seem to have this idea of the white minority being threatened as a key idea behind this zombie apocalypse in all three of these Romero films. I want to ask you if there are any cases, maybe from either Romero films or other films, where the opposite view is taken, where there is some subtext that involves the *living* as a minority, as what we think of more traditionally as a minority group, and maybe where white American culture is represented by the zombies.

Hoade: In *Dawn of the Dead*, you have—and I know we're going to talk about this in a later show, but you have the zombies coming to the mall because that's what they remember. The zombies themselves aren't really sure why they do it, but they are such consumers during their lives that in death they go "shopping" according to habit. They return to their mall, and they do this superficial shopping—never buying but always shopping—that really marks a lot of what people have to say about white America, you know? While civilization is burning, Nero may have fiddled, but white Americans would go shopping. So you've definitely got the zombies representing the white majority in that case.

FN: One more thing I want to touch on before we close out this podcast is—this doesn't quite deal with film, but I'm sure film has an example of it, too. Just in doing research for this podcast series, I came upon an interesting case from about a year ago involving a video game that deals with zombies. It's a zombie genre video game called *Resident Evil*, and it was one of the more recent installments of the game, and there was a little bit of a hubbub about this game because there's apparently a portion of the story where the white hero travels to an African village, and of course all of the zombies in that area are black because they are in Africa. They would be the dead in the area. Now, there basically was a big public outcry because being as it was a video game, your object was to kill all the zombies, who were all black in that situation. It was seen as racist and politically incorrect even though that's how it would really be in Africa. You know, you can point to the beginning of *Dawn of the Dead* as well, where, obviously, in that project house, all of the zombies (and humans) being picked off are black and Hispanic.

I wonder if there is anything to this idea that some people put forth, that maybe presenting overwhelmingly minority-race zombies (although of course they wouldn't be the miniority in Africa) is racist imagery or can be considered promoting racism? Obviously, the argument against it is they are no longer human beings and so they shouldn't be considered a race of any kind, but do you think there's anything to that? Is there danger in that imagery?

Hoade: I think that video games bear a different burden than movies do. I mean, they're similar in that you watch them and they have sound and video, but I don't know why the game designers decided they had to go into an African village at all.

They're going to a place where everyone is going to be black, and when you intentionally associate black people with this "race of creatures that aren't human," you're repeating an attitude that has been long held in American and European history. It's a horrible way to look at people, any people, so if as a game designer you're essentially encouraging players to kill black zombies in particular—and, let's face it, most people who are playing video games like *Resident Evil* are white—you've got a certain responsibility, I think, to not encourage the conflation of "zombies aren't people so it's okay to kill them" with "black people are zombies who aren't people so it's okay to kill them." There is a certain homogeneity in zombies. Except in stage of decay, they all pretty much look alike, right? And tellingly, the joke always is—that white people think all black people all look alike. It's a funny observation until you realize its implications.

Hoade: Is there something being played on there, or were the creators of *Resident Evil 17* or whatever it was actually making a rather clever comment about the video game culture and the zombie idea in general, saying, well, what if we do this? What if we have them all be black? Would that make a liberal white person less likely to kill the zombies? Would it make a racist white person more likely to play the game as a vicarious "war" against black people in general, not just zombies?

FN: Yes. I mean, it's an interesting idea. The game's developers defended themselves in the public forum by saying that there was certainly no intention to do anything racial there. But it's interesting to see the public reaction because, as you mentioned, if there were an intention to stir people up and make them uncomfortable about a scenario like that in a video game, it certainly worked.

Hoade: Yes, and then the zombies—let's say that it's this African village and it gets infected by zombiism. It's true you're not killing black *people.* You're not killing *people* of any kind. In fact, some people would say you're not even killing in the game, you're just putting the zombies down, since they are no longer alive in the first place. (And of course you aren't *killing* at all, just playing a video game.)

That said, humans are so invested in our racial divides, if you will, whether it's invested in keeping them in force or in breaking them down, that we forget, "Oh, wait, zombies aren't people! These aren't black people. These are zombies who were formerly black people, and it's hard to think that you could be racist toward a zombie.

Before we give the makers of a video game too much credit or too much blame is that these games take a very long time to develop. I would think that somebody, somewhere in the chain of command at the game developer, surely said, is this really a good idea to have this simulation of a white person blowing away undead creatures who *look like* black people? It's like shooting gallery cutouts at the county fair. You use a BB rifle, and when the BB hits the cutout and makes it fall down (and hence "killing" it). If all of the tin targets were images of black people—

FN: That carnival game wouldn't make it very long.

Hoade: [Laughs.] Right! And you're not *doing* anything to black people. There's no real black people as targets, just tin cutout targets, and shooting with a BB gun would hardly even hurt a person. However, are you not inuring players, essentially making them feel comfortable about killing members of a certain way? It's an interesting question, and that's a great thing about zombie movies and zombie games: You can ask these questions in a way that is not necessarily talking explicitly about race or explicitly about prejudice or sexism. You are talking about zombies, which is fun—but it's getting people who might not even participate in a conversation about actual racism and sexism to take part in or even open the dialogue.

And for those people who think that zombie movies or stories are just silly and maybe people shouldn't watch them because horror movies aren't very salutary or whatever, they should remember that people—young people—form their ideas not only by what their parents tell them but by what they learn from peers, from movies, from games. What are the values that are put out there? And I'm not saying that *Resident Evil* was trying to support racism in any way. I think they were just trying to develop a fun game in a setting very rarely used, but if they had thought anything about it, they might have realized they were putting forth a discussion about these issues.

Certainly, that's what Romero wanted to do. I mean, in *Land of the Dead*, you have the zombie who has kind of evolved and is now able to use a tool and think and lead the other zombies. He's a black man—a garage and gas station attendant, nothing inherently "black" or "white"—and it's perfect. Romero is purposely doing it now, and he has the credibility to get away with it and not make it seem preachy.

FN: Touching briefly on *Land of the Dead*, it's been noticed by critics that there is a wealthy "elite" human civilization which has built a fence to keep out the "undesirable" zombies. A lot of people have drawn parallels there to the United States' obsession with keeping out Mexicans and other Latinos by building a fence or a giant wall. It's almost exactly the same idea.

Hoade: Let's build a fence and keep out the Latin Americans, the Third Worlders, but also within cities. In Tuscaloosa, Alabama, where we both lived while in school or teaching, they have gated communities. The gated communities are not to keep the white people in, of course. They're to keep the "undesirables" out. This is exactly the same as Dennis Hopper's "Fiddler's Green" in *Land of the Dead*. The zombies and the poor are both excluded, and even when John Leguizamo gets the money together to move into Fiddler's Green, Hopper tells him he's still not wanted there. It's a watershed moment, and when Leguizamo is turned into a zombie, he is literally no higher or lower status to Hopper. More dangerous—maybe—but no better than any racial minority.

Romero was by this time making explicitly allegorical zombie pictures. He's saying that is the kind of society that we live in. The film is the second-worst in the *Dead* series (*Survival of the Dead* being the worst), but it's still full of symbolism and interesting parallels and things. You've got where Big Daddy, the black chief zombie played by Eugene Clark, having to figure a way into the city so that "his people" can "live" (if we want to use that term) in some kind of equality with the living, who now are truly a minority. They're literally the one-percenters, and like all unequal systems, Fiddler's Green is destined to fall sooner or later.

FN: The zombies in Land want to make a living for themselves (these words are fraught when talking about the undead, but they're the best we have). The zombies need (or at least crave) to eat, it makes an uncomfortable parallel for racists to draw. Just like in *Night of the Living Dead,* like we mentioned, it brought to mind to a lot of white people the idea that their culture, their way of life, was being threatened by a group of people (minorities) they saw as monsters constantly pushing in and invading. We have this imagery that is very prominent in a lot of American minds today that, you know, all we're trying to do is protect our way of life here in our gated-in city, protecting themselves from the mindless, soulless "monsters" pushing in from the border.

Hoade: It's exactly the parallel I think that in this case Romero was explicitly trying to make. He did it accidentally with *Night of the Living Dead,* and it was so powerful, and since then he is using that—because if a George Romero zombie movie comes out, people want to see it. It's interesting. Even if it's not great—like *Land of the Dead* isn't a great movie—they want to see it, and they want to see what he has to say, how is he going to use the zombies, and that's, I think, what makes a zombie movie worth watching for more than just cheap thrills. There are innumerable zombie movies that are nothing but monster movies, as opposed to a Romero zombie movie (and ones made by other thoughtful filmmakers) that you really take something out of and think about long after the credits roll.

Lesson 3
Zombies as Cannibals

Matt Scalici, *FilmNerds.com*: In the first episode of this series, we gave an overview of the zombie genre, and last week we took a look at the issue of race as it has been dealt with in zombie films. Today we're going to take another approach. We're going to look at the idea of zombies as cannibals and what kind of statements are made by the fact that we take for granted in zombie films that zombies are human (or formerly human) bodies eating other human bodies' flesh.

Sean, as you mentioned in the first podcast, this idea of zombies as cannibals really was not part of the zombie archetype until *Night of the Living Dead.*

Sean Hoade, Writer and "Professor Zombie": It was put in there purely to gross people out and get them to watch the movie—which it did!

FN: We've had sort-of-cannibalistic monsters in vampires, since they drink human blood, and werewolves are slightly cannibalistic in that they bite you. Certainly, people were aware of savage tribes in the jungles that were said to be cannibals, but it wasn't really until Romero that we had this idea of the dead rising and eating the living. What made Romero's use of this idea unique to 1968? Why hadn't anybody thought of it yet and what made it really stick with people back in the '60s?

Hoade: Well, you have to remember that 1968 was when the MPAA rating system first started, so you could have anything you wanted in movies really. The old production codes were thrown out the window—people were ignoring them more and more anyway—and now you could have cursing, you could have nudity, even actual pornography, and you could have violence—or at least simulated violence. If you allow something for creative people, then they're going to push that envelope before too long. So, since the exhibitors allowed extreme gross violence and blood and guts now, what Romero did was go to a butcher and got some pig guts and intestines and stuff, and that's what you see the ghouls eating out of the burning truck in *Night of the Living Dead*. By the way, the pig intestines were sitting out there all night under the hot lights and they went bad, so all the extras who ate them got food poisoning.

FN: I'm sure they did.

Hoade: Because the guts were uncooked to look real in the film, obviously. So even if those poor extras weren't eating actual human entrails, it was still pretty disgusting.

FN: That's no easy task, either, as an actor to—I mean, it's not human, but it would be tough for me if I were asked to just eat some raw animal parts.

Hoade: Yes, I know. "Here's a liver; eat this raw." I don't see that—as people have seen in the movie, though, those ghouls went to it with gusto. But anyway, cannibalism—the idea has been around for a long time and was frequently used as psychological warfare, a way to terrify your enemies. "If you resist us, we will not only beat you, we will not only defeat you, but we will then *eat* you. We will make the ultimate insult upon your person. We will actually ingest you, and then you really will be one of us. There's no more humiliating defeat."

So cannibalism was used primarily *not* for nutrition but for terrifying enemies in combat, and the tribal cannibalism we've all heard tell about is for ritual, not "I'm going to eat this because I'm actually hungry for human flesh or organs." But zombie cannibalism is *completely* different. The zombie, that's what it wants to eat. It's going to kill you, eat your organs, and then to add insult to injury—and this may be the most horrifying part—the half-eaten *you* are then going to get up and crave human flesh and brains and eat that and make other people eat it, so you're not only going to be cannibalized, but then you're going to want to be a cannibal as well, and it's the most horrifying taboo most people can even conceive of.

It's like the worst thing that you could ever be reduced to doing as a living person is to consume the flesh another person. We've seen that in the movie *Alive*, about the Andean plane crash. The shock value of that movie is that's these normal people doing absolutely the worst thing you could ever be forced to do. It's something you would only do in the most dire, no choice of circumstances, and even then some people wouldn't do it. They would rather die than do that. But get bitten by a zombie, once *you've* turned into a zombie it is the one thing you want to do: consume human flesh.

So Romero had a lot to work with there. It was already scary, the idea of these people coming after you to eat you and turn you, and you can't surrender to a zombie. The zombies aren't like one tribe fighting another tribe. You can't surrender and beg, "Please don't eat me." The zombies, if they get you, they're going to eat you, and then you are going to do the same thing with the same enthusiasm as all of the other undead.

FN: It seems like the standard surrender in a zombie movie is to shoot yourself in the head, which is not a great surrender alternative.

Hoade: [Laughs.] It's funny, though, because once you're dead, zombies lose interest in you.

They don't really want to eat you at that point—because you're not fresh? I don't know. I think the point is that it's not as horrifying anymore, not being made to *want* to do it and becoming one of *them*.

There are stories of actual cannibalism, again as an act of war terror, where they would take a captive and amputate his legs and/or arms or genitals or whatever but not let him bleed to death, and they would cook those body parts and eat it in front of him. I literally can't even conceive of the hellish horror of what that would be like. But it's *still* not as bad as being forced into wanting to do it yourself to others.

FN: So obviously, as you mentioned, what made it happen when it happened in *Night of the Living Dead* was this idea that censorship in film production was falling away and the limitations to what had always been put on what could be done in films were removed. It was at least being opened up a little bit.

So this allowed the high shock value of cannibalism on film, and it's something that almost every zombie film released since 1968 has taken full advantage of. Romero himself, as he has gone on, has included extended and more and more graphic scenes of cannibalism, to where it's down to almost this weird art of watching who can make the best scene of someone being ripped apart and eaten.

Hoade: Yes. The special effects have come so far. They aren't using pig guts anymore. Even between—you know, just in the last twenty-four hours, by the way, I've rewatched the 1978 *Dawn of the Dead* and the 1985 *Day of the Dead*, and it struck me how much advancement took place in special effects in the mere seven years between those two films.

FN: And you have really in *Day of the Dead* one of the more impressive dismemberments I've ever seen, where—

Hoade: Captain Rhodes?

FN: Yes. There's a guy that—he's actually screaming. He's screaming as the zombies start to pull his body apart, and you think, well, we've got this actor lying under the table with his head sticking up, and then the head gets removed while the eyes and the mouth are still moving, and it's not until then really that you realize that it's an animatronic head.

Hoade: When you watch it, you're not thinking, oh, that's an animatronic head. You're like, oh my God, they're ripping that guy apart.

FN: Right, yes, but it has become a little bit of a sport to zombie film lovers to see, okay, where's that big money shot in this zombie film of the guy getting ripped apart where you can really see the whole thing.

Hoade: In *Day of the Dead,* the climax of the entire movie and the money shot, as you say, is Captain Rhodes, the villain of the piece, getting ripped apart and watching his legs get dragged away, and he is going to, of course, get eaten. There isn't enough of him left to make an effective zombie.

FN: And he says, "Choke on 'em!"

Hoade: Yes, and that was an ad-libbed line! They were getting the shot, it was perfect, and then right before they pulled the very expensive fake body completely apart, the actor playing Rhodes, Joseph Pilato, he defiantly yelled, "Choke on 'em!" It was great, and they loved it and it made it into the final cut. What is amazing, though, is it was quite a risk for Pilato to do that because Romero didn't have the budget to do that whole special effect again. That's how in tune Pilato—who I hear is a terrific guy—was with this psychopathic character he was playing. "Choke on 'em!" fit perfectly with the character.

The thing is that zombies—we talk about the cannibalism, which is something that can be simulated fairly easily in film? You can just use animal parts. I mean, eating the meat of animals doesn't have to taboo of cannibalism, but it's not *that* different in actual practice.

I said earlier that zombies are the perfect movie creatures because they *do* instead of *think,* and that is what is you want in a motion picture. But they're also perfect because they're a blank slate, a hunger machine, and you can project whatever qualities you want onto them. You can say, "Oh, these actions represent racial things, and these other actions represent sexual or family things."

That's the more sophisticated approach, but we absolutely should not forget that zombie movies are intensely popular among low-budget filmmakers, including essentially *no*-budget college film students, because zombies don't really have to be played by "actors." You walk around and you moan and you are slathered in gory makeup, and essentially it's the makeup that does the acting. Maybe you eat a raw pig liver or something. But it takes no talent in front of the camera ... and actually often there's very little imagination behind the camera. That's one reason why there are so many crappy zombie movies. They're cheap, they're easy, and they titillate and disgust with almost no effort from anyone involved.

FN: The big challenge for any filmmaker or actor is creating a performance that convincingly recreates a recognizable human experience, getting something on screen that's appearing to really and truly experience something as a human being. But zombies aren't enjoying the human experience—they don't really seem to have any human experience at all! As you said, there's no motivation. There's no need for an actor in a bad zombie film to genuinely recreate any kind of condition other than this idea that they are lumbering forward looking for food, and that's really doesn't require any talent.

Hoade: Of course, in a zombie movie of any budget it's going to be scary that the undead are coming at you, but what's *really* dangerous are the other humans. They are always, *always*, going to cause the problem. If you have an impenetrable anti-zombie, fortress—it's only impenetrable if the people inside all get along and nobody decides to open a window. If somebody gets pissed at somebody else and does something stupid that lets the zombies in—which is *exactly* what happens in *Day of the Dead*—well, then you're screwed. Thus, it's the humans, the ones who *are* having genuine experiences and so must be played by actual *actors*, who are really the most frightening. I think the really low-budget, no-thought zombie movies, they forget that. They go, "Hey, we'll show zombies chewing on people for 90 minutes and people loading guns and going rock-n-roll on the undead, and that gets old really quickly.

But cannibalism! That never really gets old. In 1985, the same year as *Day of the Dead* came out, actually within weeks of its release, this movie called *Return of the Living Dead* hit theaters. *Return* was actually made by some of the people, Dan O'Bannon and John Russo, who had a hand in making *Night of the Living Dead*. In fact they got sued by Romero and those folks because of them using "Living Dead" in their title. They lost the suit because by that time, "living dead" had become a generic in the public mind.

Return isn't not actually a sequel to *Night of the Living Dead* officially, but it may have been as influential in its way than almost any zombie flick other than Romero's *Night*. It's because of this movie that everybody now "knows" that zombies want to eat brains. This is almost hard to believe now, but the first zombie movie was in 1932, 80 years or more ago, and the idea of the undead hungry for brains was introduced in *Return of the Living Dead* in *1985!* So it's actually quite new, and it's directly from that movie—a terrible movie, but incredibly influential because it's like, "Wow, they're going to eat you, that's terrible, but what if they eat what makes you *you*—your brain? They want to eat your brain. That's even more horrifying.

FN: And there's really another interesting contradiction that comes about from that in the idea that—as we know, as we've established in some of these Romero films, he always has a scientist explaining whatever it is that they think is going on, and the established reasoning, the established science behind the Romero zombies, is there is some kind of impulse in their brain that remains there that is driving them to do what they're doing, and if you destroy the brain, you've stopped the zombie. Now, this idea that you've mentioned that comes about in *Return of the Living Dead,* that zombies would eat the brains, it's oxymoronic! What creates a zombie apocalypse is the walking dead making more of the walking dead who then make *more* of the walking dead, then hungry zombies destroying perfectly good brains wouldn't seem to really help their cause.

Hoade: If the power of the zombie is in its numbers, and that comes about because zombiism is highly infectious—I bite you, you become a zombie; you bite two friends and they become zombies—*and* it's well-established that the only way you can kill a zombie is by destroying or damaging its brain, then having the zombie's motivation be to eat a living person's brain doesn't make any sense. It would be self-defeating!

If the zombies bite a person who would have become a zombie, but they eat his brain before he can get up and infect others, that would be it! There would be no spread of the zombie menace, and that wouldn't be any fun. However,

O'Bannon and Russo's idea really does speak to people because it's so horrifying to lose your locus of identity. If it's a contradiction, then as a storyteller you should probably let it go, even if it really is scary.

However, in *Return of the Living Dead* they did a couple of really clever things that I think it made the whole "brain eating" thing catch on, even though it doesn't make any consistent sense with the well-established Romero zombie trope of "damage the brain, kill the zombie." One of them is that they have a zombie actually *explain* why she wants to eat brains: It's the only thing that takes away the pain of being dead. That right there created an enormous amount of almost involuntary sympathy with creatures we formerly just felt horror and disgust for. Now, if you're dead and you're *really* dead, not zombie undead, then you don't feel any pain being dead. However, because of the toxic pollution that created the undead issue in that film, there are now reanimate dead people, zombies, and apparently there is terrible pain associated with that. If eating brains is the only thing that gets rid of that, then there is suffering. Where there is suffering, there may be human compassion. And where there's human compassion, there's a chance someone will pause when trying to kill a zombie, and then they're toast.

So that was pretty clever, considering what a crappy movie it was.

FN: At least it gives you some reasoning behind the whole "eat brains" concept.

Hoade: It gives you justification for it, so that was good, and also they made the zombie infestation occur through a chemical spill rather than Romero-esque zombie-to-zombie infection. Dead people were soaked in the graveyard by the mystery chemicals, and they came up, and then they ate the living's brains. It was different from Romero's world, though: the living did not become zombies, but all of the already-dead people (exposed to the chemicals) became zombies. Then at the end of that movie, they nuke the place to get rid of it, and all it ends up doing is throwing all the zombie chemicals up into the air into a storm system and then the implication is that the storm is going to have a huge rain, and everywhere it rains, everywhere there are graveyards—which is almost everywhere—the dead are going to rise up and go after the living. So, that movie is consistent within its own universe and quite chilling, but it doesn't really fit in with Romero's zombie idea. Even though I don't care for the *Return* universe, the idea of a cannibal that eats your brain, to me, is even scarier than a cannibal that eats just your body. That said, I would rather be dead with a chewed brain that be an undead cannibal.

FN: Because of the association, as you said, with identity and really, I guess, what some people would call the soul as being from your brain.

Hoade: It's definitely something that some cannibalistic tribes of legend did. They would eat the brains of their conquered enemies, and that would inspire even more terror. Although eating another animal's nervous system components (of which the brain is one), let alone another human's, leads to a disease called kuru in humans and scabies in animals, which is this shaking—they call it laughing disease actually or laughing sickness, and you die of it. Come to the point, it was the human version of mad cow.

So if you're a zombie and you're already dead, you don't really care if you get mad cow disease, right? But people becoming insane or literally can't stop their manic laughter, maybe that's something that audiences saw subconsciously in *Return of the Living Dead*. Eating the brains, they see all the madness and horror coming from that, so it all really ties together in a really effective way—but only in that zombie universe. In the Romero universe, brains are what run the entire show, so when they're damaged, that's the end of that zombie. Nutritionally speaking, they're no different to zombies than any other part of the body. In fact, it doesn't really make sense to eat brains for "nutrition" anyway because the brain is rather small—just three pounds or so—and it's the best-protected part of the body inside our thick human skulls.

It would just be a huge pain for your zombie teeth to try to get to that. Considering your gums are dead and your teeth are probably going falling out anyway, it wouldn't be worth it in Romero, but if it's the only thing that will relieve your pain as in *Return of the Living Dead* (1985) idea, then it's perfectly consistent that you would do that because eating flesh doesn't help; only eating the brain helps.

FN: I want to return briefly to that Romero universe and talk about *Dawn of the Dead*, which we're going to touch on in probably every podcast in this series.

Hoade: Sure. It is *the* zombie movie, and we're going to consistently come back to it, I'm sure. It's a movie that everyone always points to as criticizing American consumerism by having the zombies return to that ultimate altar of consumerism, the shopping mall. And I think there's something interesting about the the zombies' need to be constantly eating, to be constantly consuming. That's kind of the gag, the core of the commentary. You have these undead people operating completely on autopilot—they're consumers, yes, but they're not consumers like living people shopping at a mall are consumers. No, zombies are "consumers" because they're cannibals, they're consuming *people*, but it makes a nice and very funny parallel to the many people who are still living humans, not zombies, in that they are consumers, too, but of a different sort, obviously.

The humans may not be cannibals, but they constantly consume, consume, consume, just as the zombies do. What's the difference? *Is* there a difference? Lives are being wasted either way, if you think about it. My friend and colleague and zombie expert Kim Paffenroth points out that in Dante's *Inferno*, one of the worst punishments in hell isn't that you're burning or you're freezing—it's that you are doomed to repeat the same mistakes you made in life again and again and again, forever. So we have people who maybe wasted their potentially productive lives in the shopping mall when they were alive, and now that they're undead—come back to life but dead—for eternity will just keep going around and around the mall. In fact, at the very end of *Dawn of the Dead*, you've got carnival music and the very happy zombies shopping eternally, never to stop and never to be satiated, and that's a huge commentary on American and, really, with our influence on the world, world society.

FN: Sure, and I think, as you point out, the living humans really find themselves drawn to the mall as well, because they have to keep consuming as well. They have to find some way, obviously, to feed themselves, but they get also caught up in the being in the department stores. I think there are a couple scenes where they're looking at all the watches, just all the stuff they could have at the mall, as if any of that would matter at this point.

Hoade: Right, and they finally disgust themselves and realize that they have to get out of there. That's why they finally have to leave the mall or, rather, make plans to leave the mall because they're not living as humans anymore. They're see that they're no better than the zombies, and that's very powerful. You see all of the human, all of the living, characters succumb to that at some point or another, even Francine, who is saying it's disgusting that they've got the fancy watches and they're playing poker with all this money they stole out of the bank.

She judges them, since money has lost all meaning, but even she puts on pilfered makeup and preens at herself in the mirror and all the business with the fancy clothes. And when Flyboy proposes to her, in fact, in *Dawn of the Dead*, with this huge diamond ring that he got out of the jewelry store, she's like, "I can't, it wouldn't be real." If there's no cost to anything, if you can just shop, shop, shop, then any material gift *isn't* authentic. She sees that, and Flyboy sees it, too.

That's very powerful. Some people have knocked, and I think appropriately, Romero's

Dawn for its dialogue being a bit too much "on the nose," as they say, a little too much people saying *exactly* what they mean, but the characters' actions are really interesting for viewers looking at it in an existential, philosophical way.

FN: I think what it does is point people in the right direction for the conversation Romero wants us to have. Like you said, I think some people feel like maybe the comment that he makes early in the movie of, you know, "this place was important to them," that maybe that line isn't necessarily needed in the film to make that point, but you know, I think what Romero is doing is trying to everything more explicit in this film and trying to force people into acknowledging those issues as opposed to just being focused on the zombie apocalypse that's happening.

Hoade: Right, and I think some people who see the original *Dawn of the Dead* for the first time now, not that they don't enjoy it, but they're kind of like, "Oh, I thought this was just like a gory free-for-all," and they find themselves a bit disappointed that it's actually quite intellectual on a certain level.

FN: Sure, and *Day of the Dead*, as well. You mentioned it's a talkie movie. I think Romero probably heard some of the praise he was getting from the intellectual types for *Night of the Living Dead* and people appreciating some of the subtext of that, and I think he wanted to accent more of the subtext in *Dawn of the Dead* and *Day of the Dead*.

Hoade: Yes, absolutely. I mean, he's like any other person who considers himself or herself an artist. You know, you might be grateful that people are enjoying your monster movie or whatever, but usually you become an artist because you want to say something, which he did. He said, "I'm going to take this chance to actually *say* something."

Lesson 4
Zombies and Consumerism

Matt Scalici, *FilmNerds.com*: With us for the fourth installment of this fascinating series is Sean Hoade, our resident zombie expert here at FilmNerds.com and a member of the faculty at the University of Alabama.

Sean Hoade, Writer and "Professor Zombie": Thanks. This is the series that would not die.

FN: That's very appropriate! Today we're going to be talking about a topic that we have touched on in the previous podcast, but we are going to get into it in a little more depth, and that is the idea of zombies as consumers and what zombie fiction has had to say over the years about consumerism. When we talk about those two ideas converging, consumerism as applied to zombies, there's really one movie that everybody immediately turns to and that is *Dawn of the Dead,* and obviously there have been two versions of that film made and we'll be talking about both of them today.

Sean, can you briefly take us through why that is the instant connection everybody makes when we talk about zombies and consumerism?

Hoade: Oh, sure. Well, in the way that we talked about before, *Night of the Living Dead* was about race, turned out to be about race because their best actor happened to be Duane Jones, who was black. You know, it was just a serendipitous thing that happened and turned everything on its head where you can look at it and say, wow, this is about—I mean, you can look at race by looking at the concept of the zombie. This was not accidental in *Dawn of the Dead. Dawn of the Dead,* it was accidental in a certain way, but once Romero had the shopping mall idea, he knew that he could make a very trenchant but also very funny comparison between the zombies, mindless consumers of flesh, and non-zombie humans, who are oftentimes, especially in shopping malls, mindless consumers of products. How this happened was that George Romero was a very well-liked and well-respected film guy and TV guy in the Pittsburgh area in the late '70s when they were getting ready to make *Dawn of the Dead.* Because he was so well liked and so well known in the area, from making commercials and also because of *Night of the Living Dead* success, when it came time for him to, you know, I need a place to make my next zombie movie, he happened to know the owner of this shopping mall. And to your listeners who were born after the mid '70s, think of this, shopping malls haven't always been around, and the idea of taking the streets, the boulevard where you have shops and putting a roof over it so you can shop in any kind of weather, and it's always going to be open, rain or shine or snow or zombies or whatever, was a really new and interesting and, for some people, scary concept because it allowed us to really give in—I mean, there's nothing to do in a mall other than shop, other than spend money or find ways to spend money, and this is what the shopping mall is for. You're not appreciating any beautiful scenery, anything like that. You're there to consume.

So he happened to luck into this giant location, it was essentially this giant studio, where all of the—you know, most all of the movie is shot after the beginning SWAT scene and everything, and it's because he had this friend who owned the shopping mall. This gave him the idea. Once he had the location, he knew what he wanted to do with this movie. He wanted to make it into a real comment on consumerism and zombies. To his surprise, the comments that he had made, subconsciously perhaps, about race in *Night of the Living Dead* were huge, and people were still talking about it, and so this time he said, I'm going to do it on purpose, I'm going to talk about something important on purpose, and it really worked out.

An interesting note on this is that—to show you how times have changed—80% of the shops in that mall, in the Monroeville Mall, which is a real mall right outside of Pittsburgh, 80% of the shops said, sure, you can use our name in there.

FN: As bloody entrails are being dragged in front of their name.

Hoade: Oh, you guys are just having a good time, you know. The Brown Derby's in there and JCPenney and all this stuff, and they didn't have to make up any new stores, really. But in the remake, essentially no one let them use their names of logos not even Starbucks, which you'd think of as kind of the hip coffee place, not even Starbucks would let its name be used in the "hip" remake. It's all generic. Nobody wanted to touch that in 2004.

Well, not without the producers paying them a lot of money, anyway.

FN: Let me ask you this. You know, obviously part of the reason that our heroes in *Dawn of the Dead* go to a shopping mall is that it is—from a very surface plot standpoint—it's a good place to hole up. They have everything they need, but do you think that George Romero would maybe draw a distinction between our need as human beings to—you know, we do need to consume a certain amount just for survival really, not necessarily out of greed, but talk about how he makes that distinction between our need for, say, food and protection and then how it gets out of control from there.

Hoade: And our need to wear twelve Rolexes and play poker using real money from the bank thing?

FN: Right, yes, exactly.

Hoade: Well, what's funny is he handles it really well. The four main characters, they land on the mall roof, and malls were new enough at that point where people, where one of the characters, Roger, he's like, what is that? And Peter says, oh, it's one of those new shopping malls, and it looks very fortress-like. It looks very safe and fortress-like, and what they're going to do in the beginning is just go in, get some supplies, and then get out and go somewhere safer, to try to find other survivors and that thing. They stop and they do find a lot of survival—I don't know what you would call it. There are huge casks of water and all this food, this pre-packed food that can last a long time, emergency supplies, but instead of loading up the helicopter and getting the heck out of there with that, they say, hey, wait a minute, there's a lot of stuff in this mall, there's a lot of stuff we could use, we could stay here for a while and have fun and be safe from the zombies. It works out pretty well as long as they control their greed, but as soon as, of course, they get some competition for it from the biker gang, they go, "You can't take this. This is ours; we took it," and so the greed over things they absolutely don't need leads to most of them getting killed by the zombies.

FN: It's not so much that Romero is making fun of us for needing to consume things. It's when it suddenly becomes about having a good time with it and doing it to excess.

Hoade: Right, right. I think when he is having— if he's making fun of anybody, which I'm sure he is at some points, he's making fun of the people that want to have conspicuous consumption when there's no one to see it. Zombies don't care. Zombies do not care if you're wearing a gold watch or new clothes or whatever like that. They care about eating your flesh.

But they are each trying to impress each other or themselves. They simply don't know what else to do other than consume, you know? They don't know what else to do other than, well, let's go into the jewelry store and get some nice jewelry and play around and get TV while there's still TV going and make a raid on the gun store. That makes sense at least, but other than that, I mean does Francine really need makeup and a vanity and all this stuff?

If we were really faced with an apocalyptic situation like that, would we need that? Would we need those sorts of comforts? I think Romero is trying to make the point that it's silly and it's literally ridiculous, as in they should be ridiculed for it.

FN: You know, obviously it's the Romero version of this film that everybody points to as really making an impressive statement on this topic, but I want to ask you if there's anything in particular that you thought Zack Snyder did in his version that commented in a new way or an interesting way on this idea.

Hoade: Right. Well, the Zack Snyder film, I adore that movie, but other than having a shopping mall and some zombies, it really doesn't have a lot to do with the original *Dawn of the Dead*, in my opinion, because the—well, the characters are a lot smarter actually. The characters go out of their way to help—now, some of them get killed because of this, but they go out of their way to help other people that are in need, like when the truck backs up and they let them in, you know, to help the others who are survivors. Some have already been bitten and are going to be lost, especially the fat old lady, which is really scary. Of course, the character—actually played by a male stuntman in the movie—was scary probably when she was alive. But they use the mall as a—how should I say this? More as a supply closet really than, hey, we're in the mall. There's one scene where—I mean, there's one montage where they're playing video golf and they're screwing around with some stuff, but it's really kind of—they seem to want to get out of the mall, especially the Ving Rhames character. He wants to get out and see if his brother is alive at that one place, at the one shelter that's been compromised. I mean, he knows in his heart that that's gone, that his brother is gone if he was there, but he still wants to go and see, and the rest of them say, we can't stay here forever, but really there's nowhere else to go, they find out at the end.

But as far as a comment on consumerism, though, it doesn't really have—Zack Snyder didn't seem to be as interested in that. He actually seemed to be more interested in the apocalyptic implications of it, and I think that makes for a really effective movie, but it's a different kind of comment entirely—and some people were disappointed by this—about consumerism. They weren't making a comment about consumerism. They were making more a comment about apocalyptic survival, and so that's a different kind of movie. Some people took him to task. They're like, oh, it's lacking the depth of the original *Dawn of the Dead*, and you know, remakes will always get abused, but it really is a different movie. It's a different movie that's not really trying to talk about consumerism that much. It happens to be in a mall, which is still a great fortress-like place, but the mall is nowhere nearly as important to the zombies or to the people who are in it in the 2004 version as they were in the 1978 version.

FN: Maybe we should have seen that as a sign of the coming recession; they weren't as interested anymore in consuming.

Hoade: Right. Well, what's this going to be worth in a couple of years? What's the resale value on this? It's funny, though, because if you think about it, I highly doubt we're in an apocalyptic financial situation right now or anything, but if items lose their value—like a gun, if there's a zombie infestation and you have a gun, well there's something that has intrinsic value, as long as you have ammo, but rings and clothes and things like that, they don't have that intrinsic value. And what it makes you realize in Zack Snyder's version, also in the original version but even more so in the remake, is that these things never really had any value. It makes that incredibly, just really obvious and stark the way that he does that, the way that Zack Snyder presents that.

FN: And really in a way, I think there's one interesting portion... I always point to the beginning scenes before they get to the mall in Zack Snyder's version that are really captivating to me, and I think it's really interesting that he— you could point this toward consumerism a little, that the mayhem in the movie really begins in a suburb and it's this perfectly manicured little suburban division, and it's made to look ordered and perfectly—everything about it screams safety, and then as soon as this all starts going down, it's the most terrifying place you've ever seen. It's just people lunging at each other's necks and cars hitting each other.

Hoade: Complete chaos.

FN: And like you said, the value of—that people pay extra money to live in a little subdivision like that, it's suddenly all out the window; the value's gone.

Hoade: Right, exactly. I think you put that exactly right. When Ana, the Sarah Polley character in the new *Dawn of the Dead*, comes out having narrowly escaped from her zombified husband, who soon will be coming out the front door, she has the car keys in her hand and is going to the car and stops and looks up—and this is one of the reasons I like Zack Snyder so much as a filmmaker—you see her face and her utter shock and reaction before you see what she's looking at. You see her reaction first, and then you see from behind her head, you see this, you know, one of these perfect, as you say, manicured subdivisions and some houses are on fire, people are being chased all over the place, her neighbor who she knows is holding a gun on her, and then he gets hit by an ambulance, he's dead, and she has no idea what's going on. All she knows is that the safe and, if I may say about people that live in subdivisions sometimes, smug lifestyle that you might have from being so financially insulated is gone, it's gone in an instant, and not to mention—I mean, her husband is worse than dead, but he's dead, right, and you know she gets in her car and gets out and is very lucky to get out, but everything has gone haywire. You see not only has the subdivision gone down, so you've got the middle-class, upper-middle-class people are not safe. As she's on her way, you've got this metro bus that's been compromised and you've got a woman—I mean, very intentionally it looks like she's being raped, but she's not really being raped. She's just being attacked and bitten and eaten by the zombies and soon she will be one, so you've got public services like that which mostly poor people use lost immediately. As she drives away and they—what's the word? Not pan, but they zoom out, and you see that the fires and everything are everywhere, and so this menace is much larger than we thought, and you see an ambulance hit this other car and burst—I think it's an ambulance, it might just be a van—hit this other car and burst into flames. There is no safety anywhere no matter what your social standing or your wealth is, and that's all conveyed—and it also doesn't matter if you're young because we've got Vivian in the beginning, right? She's the first person that we see who is infected, and of course I love that because Vivian (her name means "life," so once she's gone, we're really in the soup. Of course, she's worse than dead— she's a zombie, so you see that it affects *everyone,* and when that truck pulls into the mall and they let the people in, already in the mall you've got people—you've got a policeman, you've got Sarah Polley, who's a nurse, you've got people who fill different roles.

You've got Mekhi Phifer as like a reformed street guy. You've got all different people, and then when they let the people in who have been injured or hiding from the zombies, they're from all different walks of life. You've got the Ty Burrell character, Steve, who's this jerk, and you've got the young girl with her dad. I mean, you've got everybody represented, and I think that he does a better—I think that Snyder does a better job with that—because that was his point—than Romero did because Romero's point was different. Snyder was saying, look, here's our little Noah's ark, the mall is like our little Noah's ark in this apocalyptic situation, and now how are the various animals going to get along together, whereas Romero was going after the consumerism which was—I mean, you can go back to the writings of Dickens and you can probably go back to the writings of Plato and find, oh, this generation is too materialistic, but Romero's idea was to show the materialism and consumerism, whereas Snyder with showing all these different kinds of people was showing that apocalyptic mentality.

FN: Right, and I think—part of it, what you touched on, I think some of it has to do with the context the movies were released in. Obviously, as you said, Romero is putting out his movie at a time when the shopping mall, the dawn of that idea, was really taking that consumerism to the next level. That wouldn't have been necessarily as much of a new idea for Zack Snyder.

FN: There is one thing that I think you've commented on in a few public places recently. There was a story in the *Tuscaloosa News* that everybody can find if you just search for Sean's name. There's kind of a wave, if you will, of the mass consumer market now having a little bit of a taste for zombie fiction.

Hoade: I like the way you put that. You know, this was not the most palatable (if you will) genre for many, many years, and I think it's becoming a little more mainstream. It's hitting with the masses a little bit more, but I want you to talk about this new wave of pop zombie fiction and where it's coming from.

Zombies, as I had said in one of our earlier podcasts, have always been kind of a movie creature because they do rather than think. They're interested in, you know, they're going to eat your brain or they're going to eat your body or whatever. They're going to turn you into a zombie. They're not so much concerned with what's my motivation and that thing. So if I say to you, "Hey, there's a zombie down the street!" what are we going to do? Assuming that you wouldn't just say I'm crazy. You'd probably say something along the lines of "We should shoot it in the head," or "We should get away from it before it bites us and infects us," right? We should make sure that people don't get near it, you know? You've got this entire cultural knowledge about "the zombie," meaning the Romero-esque zombie for the most part, to the point where you can do things like, you can make—the book that you're referring to, one of the books, is *Pride and Prejudice and Zombies*, and it's brilliant because *Pride and Prejudice* is in the public domain, you can do whatever you want with it, and so he said it's 85% Austen and 15% zombie menace, and it's incredibly well done, very clever, and the writing is very much in the spirit of Austen, with its Regency period dialogue and things like that, but now it's about dealing with zombies. Elizabeth and Jane were the most beautiful of the Bennett sisters, and now they're the best warriors of the Bennett sisters, and not only does Mr. Bennett have 10,000 a year, but he also has killed over 1,000 of the "unmentionables."

So it's very clever, but also you can do that now because people aren't going to say, "*and Zombies*? What is this 'zombie'?" I mean, everybody knows exactly what is meant when you say "zombie." Unless you're drawing some distinction like, you know, smart zombies or fast zombies or that thing, you have a status quo idea of a zombie, and now you can do things like they have young adult novels that are out. There's one called *Generation Dead*, where zombies are taking over the high school. You've got a lot of fun stuff. You've got, of course, movies. There's one called, which is funny because it's completely independent of the *Pride and Prejudice and Zombies*, but it's going to be called *Pride and Predator.*

FN: Is it basically the same idea?

Hoade: Yes, I believe so, that it's basically the Regency period, but there's—a Predator alien is there. You know, from the *Predator* movies.

It should be fun. Elton John's company is making it. Basically, it's *Pride and Prejudice*, and then an alien crash-lands, and it's, you know, Predator. It's the Predator alien. It's hilarious. It's a great idea, but—so it's the same thing where we know what the Predator thing is, but we know even better what the zombie is, and now it's just marketed. I mean, they have books, *The Zen of Zombie*, which really doesn't have anything to do with zen but is kind of about how to use zombies—how zombies act in your personal life—to do better in your business and do better in your life, and the Zen part is kind of like zombies don't think, they just do, and that's kind of a Zen idea.

It's crazy, but it's fun, you know? People can do that now, and part of what really prepped the mainstream for this were Max Brooks's books, his *Zombie Survival Guide,* which is done completely deadpan, straight-faced, and then his *World War Z,* which is an excellent piece of fiction, an oral history of the zombie war, and so it's a very sellable idea now, which of course raises the question: "Why are people buying this? Why do people want to buy stuff with realistic, plausible treatment of this fake scary menace and all this when really isn't there enough to be scared of already?

FN: Sure. I mean, I think one thing that certainly hits me going through this series and watching all these movies and as we record this here in 2009 is, you know, all you have to do is really look at a few headlines, and I'm sure everybody has been affected somewhat by some of the economic things going on, but you know it really tends to—some of the imagery and some of the hyperbole that people talk about, anything that's going on in the world today, and this is due to really just the media trying to survive, I think we're all having these apocalyptic ideas and imagery constantly pushed on us, and I wonder if maybe that has made us a little more open to these zombie stories, this idea—maybe it's hitting us on a stronger level now.

Hoade: Yes, I think so. We don't want to watch Ginger Rogers and Fred Astaire dance to "Top Hat" with all the money and everything. Let's see people having as tough a time as we are but with something different.

Also, you know, I've talked to a lot of people about zombies and people come up to me a lot of the time, oh, you're Sean Hoade, you're the zombie guy, and so they always want to talk about zombies, which is great. I love to talk about zombies, but you get this sense of excitement, especially among college guys, where it's like, I hope there is a zombie attack because I want to—you know? Because I have a plan.

It's the high ground and all this stuff, you know, and it's funny because some of these plans that people have actually could be quite effective when there's an actual real emergency.

FN: Yes. I think it's really interesting to have people fantasizing about the apocalypse and what they would do in this very specific situation.

Hoade: I mean, it used to be purely religious. The apocalypse always used to be a religious apocalypse where there would be no more suffering, you know, the kingdom of God or whomever on Earth, and things like this, and it seems like people have become less religious, not even really understanding their own religion let alone the religion of others, but they see the apocalypse as a chance to let loose, to not have to follow the everyday rules. That's part of, in the original *Dawn of the Dead*, why they can go and they're essentially robbing all the stores, right? They're not paying for anything. They rob the bank, they rob the gun store, they take all this stuff for themselves, and then they of course get mad when the biker gang comes to steal stuff from the mall because "it's ours, we took it," and that starts all the problems there. In the remake of *Dawn of the Dead*, you've got that someone dies—I don't want to give away a spoiler there— and has a boat and so they take the boat. I mean, they take it. They can do what they need to do to survive. The regular rules are off, and in that way it is like a religious apocalypse; the old ways of living are gone and we have to adapt to this new way of life and maybe it will be better, maybe it won't. It's not as clear as—if you're judged good, you go into the heavenly realm and bad you go into the hellish realm. You know, it's not quite that straightforward. Some people say, I used to say, if there's a real zombie infestation, the first thing I'm going to do is try to find a zombie and have him bite me because I want to be on the winning side.

FN: It's going to happen eventually.

Hoade: Right? I mean, it's like I don't want to be holed up in some dingy little room with nothing to eat or drink and going insane. As I talked about in an earlier podcast, it's the other humans you have to watch out for in these zombie stories, not just the zombies.

I think he did a good job of that in *Land of the Dead*—Romero, he did a good job with that, showing just the avarice and the stupidity of people. The zombies almost in that one—and some people thought he went a little overboard with this, other people thought it was just perfect, but he had—the zombies were almost noble. Zombies were doing what zombies do. They walk around and they'll bite you if they see you. Otherwise, they kind of mind their own business and shuffle around and moan and stuff like that. The people, they go and they're raiding the zombie areas and shooting the zombies, who haven't done really anything to them personally, and they're building these castles where they keep the zombies out because the zombies are the unwashed, unwanted, and it's really funny because the regular rules, they go by the wayside.

FN: And you mentioned *Land of the Dead* there. You reminded me there is actually another little mall scene I think in the big condo building we're talking about where only the rich people are allowed to live, there's a scene when everything finally does break loose and the zombies infiltrate. There's almost—you can really feel—from the way Romero puts that scene together, you can really feel he is enjoying the zombies ripping up the rich people that live in the tower.

Hoade: Yes. The rich people are really surprised, right, that this happened and they get—yes, absolutely, absolutely torn apart. They just seem so panicked because there hasn't been this slow decline there, right? There's been—you know, everything's "Oh look, life can be like it used to be," Fiddler's Green, it's just a beautiful way to live, and they've got the very clean, upscale feel to the mall, and then people are getting pressed against the mirrors and the glass and getting their necks bitten, and it's kind of amazing. Yes, you get the sense that he really enjoyed that.

Then he has *Diary of the Dead*, which shows what happens when some people are trying to—they're just trying to survive. In a way, it's a more, quote, realistic, more plausible way of looking at it, and it doesn't have that—you know, them going crazy and partying and let's use everything up since we're all going to die anyway, and it's a totally different feel. I think that that's one of the things that makes *Diary of the Dead* really worth watching.

FN: Do you fancy yourself the drunken professor from *Diary of the Dead*, Sean?

Hoade: Name the drunken, pot-smoking, lecherous professor from any movie. I want to fashion myself after Donald Sutherland in *Animal House*, but I haven't found my Karen Allen yet.

FN: I think we'll wrap up there for this week. [Laughs.]

Lesson 5
She's Not Your Mother Anymore

FN: So, Sean, one of the scariest aspects of zombies, just one of the things that inherently makes them terrifying, is that they come in the form of a human. You know, it's an image, it's a form that we're evolved to trust naturally, and in the case of zombies that all gets turned around on us, and this is an idea that was explored long before zombie fiction came to prominence. It's an idea that Sigmund Freud is actually credited with exploring called "the uncanny." Can you break that down into layman's terms for us?

Hoade: Well, Freud came up with and explored the dichotomy of the "canny" and the "uncanny," what in German he called the much more specific "Heimlich" and the "unheimlich," which translates into, respectively, something that feels like home and something that doesn't feel like home. In English, we technically would call these feelings "homely" or "unhomely," but of course "homely" has a more familiar definition of "ugly," and that's almost exactly the opposite of what Freud was saying, so we use "canny" (familiar) and "uncanny" (unfamiliar).

If you go home and your mom is baking cookies, you know, when you're eight years old and you smell the cookies and you see your mom, yes, that's great, right? That's homely.

That's canny. If you come home and what it looks and smells like is that your mother was baking cookies, but in fact she got bitten by a zombie and now there is this woman who *looks* like your mother, her moans come out in your mother's voice, and the baking cookies have been dropped on the floor—in other words, everything is the same but somehow *different,* that's the uncanny.

When, in a dream, you're at the mall, but it's *not* the mall somehow, that's an experience of the uncanny. It's where something seems and even looks familiar and yet it's *not* the same, and that is one of the most horrifying experiences that a person can have in everyday experience.

For instance, something that really scares the hell out of a lot of people is something that's completely benign, a ventriloquist's dummy. When you have a ventriloquist's dummy, it's usually like the ventriloquist is the straight man and the dummy tells the jokes, right? Well, somehow the dummy looks and acts like a person—it doesn't look *exactly* like a person, but you know, it's a caricature of a person—and yet is obviously *not* a person. Experts say that a lot of times, they will have a ventriloquist and dummy at a children's party and the kids will scream in terror and just be incredibly, incredibly afraid of this *kind of* human thing that's there. That's because of the uncanny nature of it, the *almost-but-not-quite right.* It's scary.

There was a *Seinfeld* where Jerry spends the night in Kramer's apartment, and he swears that he can hear Kramer's ventriloquist dummy, Mr. Marbles, moving around the apartment, and it's funny because I think many of us remember a fear of clowns or things that are made to look *like* humans but aren't quite right, are just a little off.

FN: That's been done in movies a good bit, too, with ventriloquist dummies and with dolls and other things like that. There's one—just in researching this, trying to keep up with my guest here on an intellectual level, which is a tough task—but there is a concept that I came upon from, I guess he's actually a roboticist. His name is Masahiro Mori.

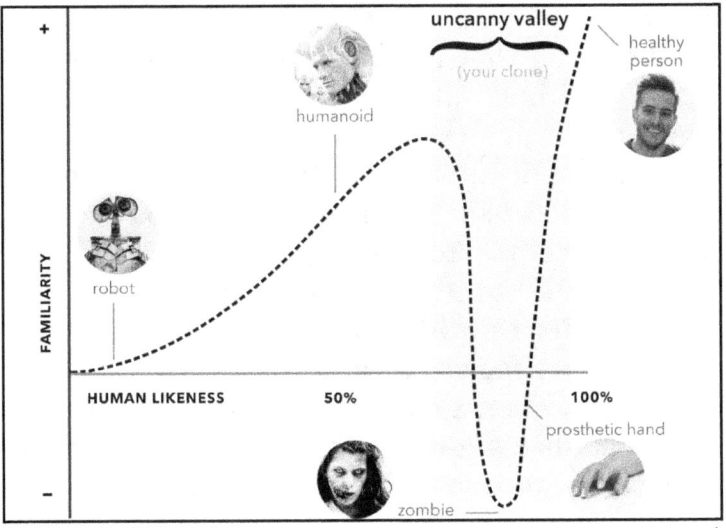

From http://blog.ionic.io/rise-above-the-platform/

He's got this kind of chart that he's drawn where as we move down one axis, it goes from an industrial robot all the way to a healthy, normal human being, and then on the other axis is how comfortable we are as people with those various things along the way. You know, we have a robot that is shaped like a human, a stuffed animal, and then there's this big dip right before you get to a normal, healthy, real human being.

Hoade: So we get more and more comfortable, but suddenly right as we approach something looking much like a healthy human being, our comfort and feelings of familiarity completely drops off the map and revulsion shoots exponentially off the diagram. And of notes Mori included on this chart, the thing that he puts on the very bottom of this "uncanny valley," as he calls it, is the *zombie*. This is what he identifies as the thing that is most like a real person yet scares the hell out of us and makes us want to vomit and run away.

The most uncanny thing that you can have is a zombie because—even more than a corpse, which is close to looking like a real living human—the zombie is even closer and thus much more revolting and frightening. You're slightly less fearful of a corpse than a zombie, you know? Even a corpse doesn't bring this kind of fright that a zombie would, and that makes sense, because a zombie is more like a real person because it moves. But it ain't *right* somehow.

I think Mori is on to something there. They talk about they are trying to make humanoid-looking robots, and it's funny because the closer they get—if it's cute and doesn't really look that much like a human, you know, like C-3PO in *Star Wars*. People *love* C-3PO—he's so adorable and funny! But he's a golden-metal robot with stiff movements, not that human-looking at all. Let's say he looks 60% human in that he's a talking biped with symmetrical, quasi-human features. But if you build a humanoid-type robot something that looks *99 percent* human, it produces these feelings of fear and disgust until you get to that 100 percent, and that's a problem that researchers trying to make a convincing humanoid robot (*android,* technically, "man machine") have run into. It's like the closer they get, the more they give people the creeps.

These robotics geniuses are brilliant at making their robots looks more and more human-like, particularly, the latest generation of Japanese robots. They get more and more human-looking, and you could show these YouTube videos to anybody, and the first thing people say is, "Wow, look how human that thing looks!" But then it's often followed up with "Oh my god, that's one of the scariest things I've ever seen."

Something's not right there, and that's exactly what vexes the roboticists. There's a lot of ... well, if you put nerds into any situation, soon thoughts will turn to sex, okay? And it's perfectly normal, I suppose, but there is a book out called *Love and Sex with Robots,* which examines this phenomenon, and to a nerd, this would seem to be the perfect thing! Because you could make your robot or whatever as sexy as you want it to be, and you can do any nasty things you want with it, but you don't have to talk to it, which would maybe be a nerd's—not a *film* nerd—but a nerd's dream.

In fact, if people have seen *Fido,* they know that the human character played by Tim Blake Nelson has as his companion—his *pet,* if you will—a zombie, and she was very hot and attractive, too much so to be with a weasel like Nelson's character. She had died of some natural illness or whatever and was brought back as a very well-preserved zombie. So she basically looks like a normal person, except she's got that kind of vacant look and a little bit of blood around the mouth, I guess from feeding. And it's *so* creepy to audiences, because you know that Nelson uses this thing for sex. The idea of having sex with a dead body, necrophilia, is sick enough, but then a zombie where it's dead but in a way able to know what's happening to it—that's even sicker and weirder because it's even *more* uncanny.

In *Fight Club*—I don't know if it's in the movie, but it's in the book—there's a woman who has terminal cancer, and she's in the later stages of it, and her skin is kind of yellow and tight against her skull, and she's basically begging for somebody to come and have sex with her, to give her a little bit of pleasure before she goes. But even just reading it, you feel repulsed because she is not a healthy human. (Chuck Palahniuk is brilliant at creating scenes of disgust and horror that act as a mirror on our own sick selves.) She's not quite—and this is not anything against, you know, people with diseases or anything—but in the idea of the uncanny, she is a little bit off, and so she provokes that fear and disgust response. I don't think anyone takes her up on her offer, sadly.

However, we're not talking about a prejudice, conscious or unconscious. It's that, on that Freudian, psychological level—and even more on the Darwinian level—we want to mate only with the most healthy specimens so our offspring will also be healthy. We are disturbed when something looks a little bit less than a healthy person, which is obviously what's the case there. And something that looks *dead* but still walks around ... despite Nelson's character in *Fido*, I don't know anyone who would screw a zombie.

When you have a zombie, you have the least healthy that a person can possibly be. Even less healthy that just being a corpse.

Yet they still, in the beginning at least before they start rotting, look like Grandma or they look like your boyfriend or your girlfriend or your brother or your sister or whatever, but they're not, they're not. You know, that's not your mother anymore.

She's not your mother anymore, as they say in *Night of the Living Dead,* yet, wow, she looks like her, she's wearing the same clothes. Five minutes ago she *was* my mother and saying she loves me and all that, but that's what makes it incredibly uncanny because she's so close, *so close* to being the person who loved you and whom you loved.

Readers should check out the diagram reproduced above, where right before healthy person is *zombie,* at the very nadir of familiarity and comfort. It then zooms all the way up because a healthy person is familiar and they're not creepy and don't produce fear responses and things like that. That can be kind of a gross discussion.

FN: What we're talking about gets a little more disturbing when we aren't talking about just any human, but we talk about a *specific* human being who you know suddenly is *not* that specific person—or *any* person, really— anymore, and this is an idea that you'd be hard-pressed to find a zombie movie where it isn't explored.

There are a few films that I want to touch on particularly, including *Shaun of the Dead,* a 2004 entry in the genre. To me, it really does one of the better jobs I've ever seen at putting you through on a psychological level what it would be like to have a loved one suddenly fall from the canny mountaintop into that deepest trench of the uncanny valley. How do think *Shaun* so effectively deals with that idea?

Hoade: Well, in *Shaun of the Dead*, his stepfather, his mother, his best friend, other people whom he knows, one of his roommates, all of them get turned into zombies during the course of the movie. And he has to shoot his mother, with whom he is very close, but it's *not* his mother anymore. He has a truly hard time dealing with that and accepting that. On a certain level, I mean, he does shoot her, so he knows that she's a zombie and isn't in fact his mother anymore. But in another sense, she was so dear to him and so affectionate of him, calling him "Pickles" and all this stuff, that it's really difficult for the audience, too. And he *doesn't* end up having to shoot his best friend, and that friend keeps enough of the human in him to want to play the video games and everything. Forever.

FN: That's a little bit going back to the *Dawn of the Dead* idea, when the zombies keep going back to the mall, a place and activity they were most familiar with. Kind of a reference to that.

Hoade: That's one of the reasons why I think that *Shaun of the Dead,* while being extremely funny and a great comedy, is also a very unnerving zombie movie. It really goes into that uncanny idea: It's not just that you wake up in the morning, like in the 2004 *Dawn* remake, and your next-door neighbor's little girl is coming to the house and she's a zombie and she's trying to kill you, horrifying as that is. It's also—or maybe even moreso—that when the protagonist, Ana, steps out her front door. It is her neighborhood, but then it *isn't*, because her neighborhood doesn't have all the buildings on fire and people getting run over in the street and dead people running after each other and screaming and all this stuff. It's *technically* the same place, but it's different, and that's the intensely unsettling sense of the uncanny: the closer it seems to normalcy but doesn't quite make it, the more horrifying it is.

One of the things about *Blue Velvet*, David Lynch's masterpiece from 1986, is that Kyle MacLachlan finds a human ear on his lawn, on the *lawn*, an encroachment into his canny existence and shooting it right into the uncanny because his neighborhood is not quite what he thought and felt comfortable with. You know, Lynch was going to have him find a finger, but they decided that somehow an ear would so much more intimate, so much more *invasive* into the character's misplaced sense of safety and well-being. What he sees, and it only takes a nanosecond, is that this white-picket-fence, this little Opie-Taylor-and-Huckleberry-Finn world that he thought he was living in, has all this horrible stuff going on behind it. He had never seen it that way, but now he sees it in a totally new and different way, and it's incredibly, nauseatingly frightening to him.

FN: David Lynch loves messing with the uncanny, that's for sure. You know, like I said, I think probably every zombie movie has some instance of this, but we were talking about *Diary of the Dead* in the last podcast, and I think it has a particularly effective scene along this line. I'll say this—I hadn't seen *Diary of the Dead* until I was doing research for this podcast series—it's not the best-written zombie movie you'll ever see. Romero maybe struggles a bit with writing teenager dialogue, but that's understandable from a man in his 60s in 2008, when that film was released.

There is one particularly nasty scene that really gets me: it's where the main heroine of the story goes back home. She's been trying to get in touch with her family for the entire film up to this point, and then they get to her family's house and realize that something's gone wrong, but they don't quite know what. (They don't know about the zombie apocalypse about to happen.) It's pretty much the worst-case scenario, the worst thing she could've seen, when she comes in. *Something is … wrong.*

Hoade: It's all because with the uncanny, Freud's uncanny, everything is *so close* to being right and familiar and yet it's not quite there. If I see an army of skeletons instead of an army of recently dead zombies, that's scary, right? But it's scary at a wholly different magnitude to say, "Oh, there's my high school principal and there's my wife and there's my best friend and they're all coming to eat me, they're all coming to kill me," than to see just these anonymous skeletons. Skeletons would be plenty scary, but seeing the people that you love and who would never hurt you and whom you would never hurt suddenly turned into a "you kill them or they're going to kill you" situation makes it infinitely scarier.

Interestingly, Freud made the connection between the uncanny in our dreams and the uncanny in jokes. This may seem a little bit off the topic, but it's all with the uncanny because our dreams seem symbolic a lot of times, and what they do is—what it seems that the mind does, according to Freud, is couches our real feelings about things in the uncanny so it's not quite—we're not thinking it quite directly, so it's able to get around the censor of the superego, you know? If you're having lustful feelings toward your second cousin, but you're in denial that's very deep, well, maybe in your dream you see her and you in a space capsule or something, and it's not sexual at all in the dream, but the symbolism, maybe of a phallic missile launching launch and a splashdown in the wet ocean—

FN: You've got a dark turn of mind, Mr. Hoade.

Hoade: [Laughs.] Well, you know, much of Freud's work is about the subconscious and how recognizing relationships between fantasy and reality can relieve the tension of holding reality back, and it's the same thing with jokes. It's like, many people have ethnic jokes, people who don't see themselves as prejudiced. But the joke is found funny even if it's an ethnic or racist or sexist joke (and therefore "wrong") because everybody who is not of that certain ethnicity or gender probably harbors certain fears or negative feelings about people of those ethnicities that one just doesn't talk about in polite society. In fact, many probably don't even admit it to themselves, so when that person tells such a joke, you have this uncanny disconnect, because it's not exactly reality the joke is referring to, but something close enough to amuse but not threaten, and that relieves a lot of the tension.

In the same way, coming back to zombies, we have a distinct fear of death, most humans do. We, at least in the Western world, have a very sanitized view of death. We almost never see a corpse in its natural state, and we can't admit that we're scared of those things, because people just don't talk about that. So in zombie movies, where characters *have* to deal with the dead in this impossible way, you're using the zombie situation in this uncanny sense since it's *not* exactly what life is like. It's close to it, so it's scary and vicariously fun, but in fact Freud would say that you're actually dealing with your feelings about death by watching zombie movies, your feelings about decay and mortality. This is using Freud's uncanny in a way that maybe the filmmakers weren't even aware of! They weren't aware of what they were doing, which is why God invented us academics to help them out.

FN: [Laughs.] So we can dig up what George Romero didn't even know he was talking about.

Hoade: Right. It's the whole purpose of academia, to figure these things out. Plato himself would have said the end result would be figuring out how horror movies do what they do, and why.A movie that I recommend that everyone who is interested in zombie films should see, because it really, really plays up this idea of the uncanny, is *Zombie Honeymoon*.

In *Zombie Honeymoon*, it's not like a zombie infestation or anything like that. This husband and wife are on their honeymoon, and they're on the beach, lying out, and this person in a wetsuit and a diving mask comes out of the water and something is obviously wrong with him. He staggers up and in a *28 Days Later...* kind of way and vomits this black bile onto the man and then dies. The man—this is disgusting, of course, but he cleans himself up and everything seems fine ... but soon he starts to get sick. His sickness is not only that his skin starts decaying, and things like that, but also that he starts getting this taste for human flesh. He tries to deny it to himself at first, but then he ends up killing someone—not his wife—and eating them bit by bit while he keeps the body in the bathtub. The wife finds this and, like anyone when you get married and you don't really know the other person that well—I mean, you get to know somebody better all during your life together, but you never know them *perfectly*— she's trying to accept it and rationalize it in the same way that someone might say, "Okay, all right, I don't necessarily like that my husband likes to play golf every weekend with his friends, but I can work with it.

This whole thing is naturally kind of disappointing to her, but how is she going to work around it? Well, in her case, it's "Okay, my husband is starting to rot and has a taste for human flesh. How can I help him and our marriage through this? Not necessarily help him *kill* people, but how can I make him feel loved and appreciated and all this when really the only thing on his mind right now is being a zombie." So it is amusing in its way, but what it really is—what the whole movie is really about— is watching someone who you know become something different, and so you move from the canny, the familiar, to the uncanny and the unfamiliar. As he changes from her regular human husband into this zombie, she loses him. And that's frightening to everyone, to have someone you know be replaced by this completely unfamiliar thing that's there.

Really, the metaphor they're making is like if people are in a relationship and one of the partners gets a terminal disease, a wasting disease of some kind. It's the same person, but it's *not* the same person. It's no longer the familiar; it's unfamiliar and horrifying, and horrifying for both people in the relationship as they see things enter the uncanny valley of disgust and revulsion.

Zombie Honeymoon is a low-budget movie, but it's extremely intelligently made. The actress who plays the wife, Tracy Coogan, is really excellent. The acting on her part is quite convincing for a low-budget genre movie. Anyway, that whole movie is about moving into the realm of Freud's uncanny, and you watch it happen. It's not like a person wakes up one morning and Grandma is a zombie. The husband *slowly* changes into this thing that isn't what she married and isn't what she knows. It looks familiar and speaks in a familiar way, but it's not her husband. You know, "It's not your mother anymore," that kind of thing.

FN: Yes, I think that's one interesting thing about zombie movies like this. In most zombie films we have, you know, you're alive—even if you've been bitten, you die like a person would normally die just from anything—and then you have this moment where you wake up and you're a zombie. It's interesting to have a film that deals with it on a gradual level because that accentuates, like you said, that idea of the uncanny, because you're having to deal with the slow pain of experiencing that loss in increments, and like you said, you can draw a parallel to maybe a terminal disease or an addiction or something like that.

Typically, when we talk about the uncanny, we are also talking about the grotesque, about horror-type ideas, but obviously that same phenomenon that happens in our brain that makes us disturbed at those images is what's working when we see someone we love become less healthy, in a way less *human*, over a period of time.

Hoade: Horror movies wouldn't be scary if they didn't remind us of real life in *some* way, you know? If there weren't a certain amount of fear of the transgressive nature of a teenage roll in the hay, if there weren't already a fear of doing something that's not allowed, then the *Friday the 13th* movies wouldn't exist.

If we weren't really afraid of death or afraid of losing those who are familiar and important to us, zombies wouldn't be scary to us. Gross, maybe, but not scary. Zombie movies are very rarely about you yourself getting killed or bitten. That would be bad enough, but it's the people that you see, the survivors, who make it so horrifying because those people, their existence in a desperate situation, are what we can relate to the most. I think that is the entire reason that the zombie genre continues to grow in popularity year after year after year. I mean, the phenomenon just continues to explode. It's amazing ... but not quite as amazing when you realize that people's fear of death is definitely *not* fading. I think filmmakers are becoming more skillful at tapping into that, going beyond the surface blood and guts (but still including them, of course) into what *truly* frightens us.

Lesson 6
Zombies as Modern Fears

FN: Hello and welcome back to FilmNerds.com. I'm your host, Matt Scalici, and we are continuing our a look at the zombie genre with zombie expert Sean Hoade.

Hoade: [Laughs.] "Zombie expert." I'll be the person with the pipe that they'll turn to when the zombies actually attack.

FN: Excellent. Yes, you'll be the last thing people see on their television feeds.

Hoade: Right. It's gonna be like, "It's just logical, it's logical," and I'll be rubbing my eye patch.[1]

FN: In this segment we're going to be looking at modern, contemporary fears and the way that the zombie genre is tapping into some of those today. Every effective horror movie works, on the one hand, by having a good screenplay filled with tension and scary images and things, but the *really* good ones seem to tap into something that's a societal type of fear, something that is especially germane to the time that the film is released. We've talked about in this series before how the zombie films of the '50s and '60s touched on this underlying fear of the culture wars and also the idea of African-Americans and

---

[1] In order to get this joke, watch the 1978 *Dawn of the Dead*.

other minorities entering into the "territory" of the racist white majority, and other horror films have addressed things like nuclear war and other kinds of contemporary fears.

The zombie genre has put out some interesting films in the last ten years that play on our fears in the post-9/11 world. Obviously, Sean, it hasn't been a difficult decade to scare people when it comes to these kinds of things. Talk about some of those fears that you think are pressing on society today and then the way that the zombie genre has approached some of those.

Hoade: Yes, sure. Well, what's true about the new millennium is we have many real things to be scared of. Even though full-out nuclear war is a lot less likely than it was perhaps in the mid '80s or so, the chance of a nuclear attack, like somebody just setting off a single bomb, seems a lot higher because those weapons and codes seem to be in a lot of different hands. So our fears are different. Despite that, these fears don't necessarily interfere in any way with how we live our lives, except maybe trying to get on an airplane at the airport.

We have a general sense of complacency. We go to the mall. We go to school. We go to our jobs. Things don't really seem that scary. It's not like during the blitz of 1940 in Britain where every night you're thinking, "Am I going to get bombed and killed tonight?" So we turn to our horror movies, or our horror movies turn to us, to give us this vicarious feeling of fear, to shake us a bit from our complacency and remind us that there's still a lot to be scared of out there. But why horror films that do this are enjoyable because they don't give us a one-to-one correspondence with the real fear out there, instead using what's lurking under the surface in our minds to make what they *do* portray absolutely horrifying.

When the first zombie movie came out, *White Zombie* in 1932, that was a time of military interventionism in Haiti, and many Americans were wondering what we were doing there. Haiti was this exotic place, "primitive" to our eyes, so how would the Haitians fight back against this invasion? Because eventually, we know that whatever culture is subjugated is eventually going to fight back, and so here comes the bogeyman, the Haitian zombie.

In the '50s, of course, there *was* the constant fear of nuclear war and nuclear fallout, and with those, fear of your neighbor, since that family could be spying for the Communists. But if there *is* a nuclear war and your neighborhood survived and you have a shelter and some supplies, your neighbor—maybe even that neighbor you suspected of being a Red—will come knocking pretty soon, maybe with a gun. It's no coincidence that in the 1950s producers created movies like *The Zombies of Mora Tau*, where for the first time there's a *literal* a contagion of the zombie disease. Being friends with people who turn out to be Communists could make you look like—or even actually become—a Communist yourself, just through exposure.

Then you get into the 1960s, where, as we've said, many people both black and white suffer from fears of racial issues exploding. In the 1970s was the first widespread fear that we're all becoming completely shallow consumers who go to mall instead of church on Sundays and so forth. Then, in the 1980s was the unprecedented military expenditures and buildup of the Reagan years, so you get *Day of the Dead*, scientists vs. soldiers. The 1990s brought the world intense fear of biological war and terrorism, so what's really been a huge step forward for the zombie genre has been this idea of mass contagion, a natural or manmade epidemic or pandemic. This is a fear now ingrained in us, and some people don't even realize that's what they're scared of when they get scared of the wildly contagious and maleficent zombie menace. Now, in the first years of the twenty-first century, all of those fears have come together in many people's minds, and not surprisingly the zombie craze has grown like never before. We have the terrorists, usually people of a different race, who believe in "magic" through their religion telling them to kill. They can explode atomic or dirty bombs or set off biological weapons and infect or kill us all, and these combined fears are often fully addressed only through the Romero-esque zombie mythos.

FN: Obviously, epidemic viral disease has begun to serve as the go-to explanation for any zombie apocalypse in the movies, instead of having it caused by radiation or—isn't there an alien-type explanation in *Night of the Living Dead?*

Hoade: Right, right. Actually, yes, the probe comes back—and Romero never explicitly connects it, which makes it even better—the probe has returned from Venus and crashed, and apparently it's brought along with it some cosmic radiation. It's concurrent with the dead rising, and so NASA is being consulted. We are left to believe—but never know—that it's something extraterrestrial, some kind of space disease or Venusian radiation is making the dead rise. Then, of course, the best part is always that the dead rise and then make other people dead and then they rise. Damn those Venusians!

FN: Sure. I think, like you said, part of what has changed with the genre is the scientific explanation, actually the *pseudo*-scientific explanation, now given with every zombie crisis. One that pops into my mind is Danny Boyle's *28 Days Later...*—it's probably the best example in the last ten years of the epidemic-disease fear really used very directly in a zombie movie, and I think you've said you *do* consider that a zombie movie, even though these people aren't reanimates.

Hoade: Oh, definitely, yes. I think the fact that the people aren't actually dead, that's irrelevant. I suppose being dead *is* part of the definition of a zombie, with the rotting flesh and all that stuff. Looking at it through the lens of the uncanny we talked about last time, even though the afflicted in *28 Days Later...* and *28 Weeks Later* are not technically zombies—they didn't die and come back—they still are uncanny as hell. It's your mother one minute, but then she gets the Rage Virus and the next minute it's this glassy-eyed, homicidal maniac who's trying to infect and kill you, *definitely* not your mother anymore. So really, I think at the time when your best friend is bearing down on you, trying to vomit bile into your mouth to turn you into this thing with no free will that just wants to attack and feed, the ontological niceties of the situation are lost. "Well, is this really a zombie that's attacking me? Or is it just a person who is ill?" I think it ceases to matter.

What happens is that we have no idea what sick stuff our government or private groups or terrorist groups have come up with as far as infectious agents, and so that frees our fears to run free. And what better way to let them run free than to make a horror movie or a science fiction movie? Because that has been the way, for the past hundred years, that you can comment on the times without attracting the official or unofficial censors. "This is just entertainment. We're not *really* commenting on anything important."

Yet the unease that you have, to say the least, when you're watching *Friday the 13th* and you're seeing young people being punished for indulging in the newly societally accepted sexual promiscuity—indirectly punished, but you do see them being punished for that—you are seeing our unease in society with that "transgressive" behavior. And so when, in a zombie movie, you see people getting infected and it's this pandemic suddenly sweeping the country and then the whole world, you are seeing your fears about contagion made literal, completely realized.

I mean, we're all so closely packed together—we're the most closely packed together that we've been since the walled cities of the Middle Ages, and we should remember that the Black Death affected mostly city dwellers, rich *and* poor, because that's where the highest population concentration was, and so the fleas that carried it were passed around very easily. The people out in the country, they were much less affected. So once again we have this incredible, incredible concentration of populations, now not in cities but over entire continents, which is perfect for any kind of pandemic story, but especially a zombie one.

FN: I'm not sure if this is a conscious thing or if I'm just reading into this, but I've noticed in the more recent zombie films, especially the ones in the last ten years, there's almost always a scene in a hospital where things have gone really wrong. And I think that might play into a fear of a badly equipped emergency response system, an unreliable health system, all the things we lean on in times of trouble. If something like this were to break out, you'd think, "Well, let's go to the hospital," but if you look at Zack Snyder's *Dawn of the Dead*, it has a hospital scene, *Diary of the Dead* has a hospital scene, and also *28 Days Later*.... There's very frequently a scene where the hospital is seen in operation at the beginning of the film, but soon it's become completely abandoned and useless.

Hoade: Completely devastated, right? Yes, it's interesting because of a couple of things. Max Brooks, in his brilliant *Zombie Survival Guide*, said places people would think to go when there's an emergency would be either hospitals or police stations, and he said—you know, he treats it wonderfully deadpan and serious through the whole book—that those are the two places you absolutely should *not* during a zombie crisis because everybody's gonna go there.

Some percentage of those people at those places is going to be infected, and they'll turn, and then everybody else will get infected, and so those are literally the most dangerous places you can be. Now, Brook's book is of course a work of fiction and created for fun and everything, but in the real world there was a scientific poll that asked health workers, doctors, nurses, orderlies, you know, all kinds of health workers: If there were a highly contagious pandemic like a super Avian or bird flu, would you go to work? Would you go to work at the hospital where you know there are going to be all these sick people? *Seventy-three percent* of the people said no, they would *not* go to work. I don't blame them, either, because the second people to get infected are always going to be the doctors and the nurses and the cops. The professional helpers. And when the helpers are gone, by definition, the rest of us have no one who knows how to help us.

And so that's another fear that we have. Tens of thousands of people who check into a hospital every year die of some infection that they picked up *in the hospital*. So really, even now hospitals aren't necessarily seen as these health sanctuaries. They're seen as actually very dangerous places that you go to only if you absolutely have to.

FN: I've wanted for a while to ask you this as our resident zombie expert. Since you mentioned the hospital and the police station turning out specifically not to be good places to go, if a zombie epidemic hits, Sean, where would you go? I'm *sure* you've spent some time thinking about this.

Hoade: Where would I go? Yes, I have definitely devoted thought to this.

FN: Oh, I know I've thought about it.

Hoade: Exactly. Everybody says, "Oh, well, you seek high ground and you try to find a place with lots of weapons" and things like that. A lot of people say they would go straight to Walmart because those stores have weapons and other supplies, pretty much everything you'd need to lay in and wait out a siege, but of course everybody else is going to be thinking that same thing! Soon all the canned food is taken and all the guns are gone and so on. You know that somebody who is infected will be in there, too, and then all hell's gonna break loose.

I think the best thing to do in any kind of pandemic/epidemic situation, including zombie attacks, is to just *already* have supplies—food, generator, wind-up radios and flashlights, weapons—and hole up in your home. Don't go out. And certainly do *not* leave to go try to save anybody else. Don't say, like they do in almost every zombie movie, something like, "My mom must be stuck at the grocery store! I *have* to go get her."

I mean, it's a trope that just seems to have a real ring of human truth to it. But as compassionate as we want to be, we're not doing *anybody* any favors by going out and getting infected ourselves, so the story's, you know, "Mom went out to the grocery store" or, "Oh, my sister lives just across town, I've got to get to her and bring her to my safe place." You know, "That's where they said there were a bunch of zombies, so I'd better go over there and save her." Number one, if she is among a concentration of zombie she is very probably already one of the zombies and, number two, *you* will very, *very* likely become one of the zombies yourself if you try to blast your way into a highly concentrated area of zombie infestation. The best thing to do is save yourself by staying quiet in your bunker. If everybody just tried to save themselves, then a lot more people would stay people a lot longer, I think. Of course, that's what you do in a zombie movie because it creates suspense and anxiety. In life, those would be two of the less-fun emotions to experience.

What's funny about this, though—or maybe not so funny—is that we're talking about this because this is a podcast about zombie films and zombie stories. We naturally talk about "This is what you do in a zombie invasion"—it's sort of a deadpan joke, ha ha, right? But actually it's also excellent advice in *any* kind of real emergency situation. Any of these other things that we're talking about, these modern fears, you can often apply them exactly to the zombie disaster scenario.

It maps exactly, and that's why zombie films and stories are so effective and scary. It's because there's a one-to-one correlation of real-life things that can and will happen, and so we can go, "Ooh, zombies are scary," but then if there's an actual pandemic—and one day there probably will be, there have been many before—you've got your survival plan already worked out. You should have food, you should have water, you should have entertainment so you don't lose your mind and go stir-crazy and start killing people and things like that. If there's a riot going on, the safest place is in your house. Don't try to get away. Your car in motion is much less safe than your house planted in the earth.

Again, though, if somebody wrote a zombie story that had people sensibly staying in in their houses, that wouldn't be a very interesting story. Even *Night of the Living Dead* needed those two dumb hick teenagers to go out to fill up the truck. Then *BOOM*—the truck is destroyed and the hick kids get eaten. Just stay in the house.

There are exceptions to this rule in zombie or disaster or monster movies. They did a nice job of this in *Cloverfield*, with the huge Godzilla-like monster wreaking havoc in New York. "There's the girl that I love, we just had a fight, and she's across the town, and now the monster's attacking. I've got to go just let her know that I love her, you know. Even if it gets me killed, I have to know that she's alive and tell her that I love her." That's a very human thing to do and makes for an exciting story, but it's *not* the way to survive a monster attack.

FN: In fact, it gets both of them killed in the end.

Hoade: Yes, it does. I mean, they wouldn't have been in that helicopter in Central Park when the monster jumps up and smashes it. They would have gotten the hell out of Dodge. So "being a hero" works for that. I mean, I don't think we're really scared of monster invasions the way that back in the '50s Americans were like, "Hell, are the Russians going to invade? Are we going to invade Russia?" There was a real fear of actual, literal invasion, and it had only been ten years at the most since Hitler had essentially had his way with the European continent, so those fears were really fresh and salient, but could only safely be expressed as, "Oh my gosh, this big monster is going to invade our city and get us. With the death of the Cold War, we're not afraid of human or giant monster invasion but about invaders that are microscopic organisms, literally too small to see.

We as a species have perverted nature in such a way that honestly if there were something real that were like zombies or the Rage Virus where I lose my free will and also become incredibly aggressive, it could something that the Army would like. Creating super soldiers! If that happened, people would be horrified, but I don't think they would be completely surprised. In fact, when the SARS epidemic was going on in like 2004, there was a worldwide panic. People were walking around with those doctors' masks on their faces. Travelers weren't allowed to fly to the United States from Singapore. I mean, it was *complete*—everything was shut down because there's this disease that's going to wipe us all out. Well, 774 people ultimately died of SARS. Not that those lives aren't very important, but that number is about half of the people who died on the *Titanic*.

It definitely was not an epidemic. It wasn't out of control. Yet the way it spread was so fast and unexpected that more than one commentator likened it to a zombie infestation. It's like, "Oh no, I was exposed to this person, now I have this disease! I'm going to die! Anybody that gets exposed to me is going to get it, so stay away or you'll die, too!"

It's incredibly scary in these movies because it's perfectly relevant. There will be definitely another—many more—pandemics, but never have there been *so many people*, so history is no longer a guide to how it's going to work out. To deal with those fears, I'm going to make something to scare the hell out of people. I'm going to make a movie about a pandemic. Well, okay, you have that movie *Outbreak* with Dustin Hoffman and Rene Russo, which was a piece of crap. It really wasn't scary.

A movie where I get it and I get sick and I die, I mean, that's not fun, and that *is* scary in its way. But it's not as scary as a disease makes you attack the people that you love and trust the most or makes them attack you, so it's "I'm going to make a movie about pandemics! I'm doing zombies!"

By the way, here's what separates good or great horror movies from horror movie sequels. In the original, there was the desire to creatively make a comment about what's going on in the world today. You do it through horror, you do it through, "Wow, my next-door neighbor is a stranger to me." That is the case for most people in the urban environment, right? Well, what if he's *literally* a stranger in that I know him so little that to me he's barely human? Like Michael Myers. "I know the people around me so little that they might as well be wearing masks and coming to kill me for no reason."

However, when the money is all that matters, when they just cash in on the powerful original story, when you make *Halloween 17* and Michael Myers has become this superhuman monster—same thing with *Friday the 13th*, you know, Jason Voorhees has become this superhuman monster—it's like, "Meh, you know, it's not really scary anymore," because it's not making any particular comment about anything. It's not trying to tap into anything real—not any kind of fear, not even tapping into anything in the Zeitgeist.

I mean, as we talked about a few episodes ago, *Diary of the Dead*, the fifth Romero zombie movie and one that I liked much, much more than *Land of the Dead*, used as its anchor of reality the YouTube generation and the Instagram-Vine-Tumblr-Twitter phenomenon, this brave new world instant information, instant messaging, which isn't necessarily anything scary. I mean, YouTube isn't *scary* in that way, right? But what Romero did was he inserted his zombies and used the zombie apocalypse to illustrate the prevalence and the pervasiveness of this YouTube culture, Facebook/Twitter thing, which at that time (2010) many people weren't even really noticing as a generational issue. I think it worked really well. It wasn't even about a fear *per se*, but he used a highly fearful situation to comment on the phenomenon.

FN: Right, and it gets grim, more than scary, because you get this sense in the end that all these people who are somehow surviving this are just—who are they even commenting to? A little bit like in *Dawn in the Dead*—who are they all dressing up for? Who are they trying to impress? These kids are posting and editing their movie to make it a little sharper, a little cooler, but it's like, who's going to be left to watch this movie?

Hoade: Yes, and *Diary of the Dead* has one of the most effective endings in zombie film, where the main girl is watching the video that someone has posted where they've tied a female zombie up by her hair, and they're just shooting at her and eventually blow her head off, and then there's just the top of her head left, attached by the ponytail.

And the character is like, what kind of people have *we* become? Forget about the zombies— are *we* people who should even survive? Because those are the humans, the living people, who are doing that to the zombies who are—yes, they'll bite you and attack you and all this stuff—but are helpless, really. They cannot choose to do other than what they do, but humans *can* choose to do otherwise, do things other than be cruel, but so many times we don't choose to do that. We choose to spend our time like, "Let me find the most horrifying accident video on the Internet, and I'm going to watch that over and over and vicariously take part in this actual person's tragedy."

I think Romero, who has always been a keen social observer, just does a great job with that. Thirty years ago, the Internet as we know it was just getting started There was DARPANET and everything, but the Web and such as we know it was just getting started. Who knew that there would be this kind of civilization where we're all connected all the time, not just in science fiction but in reality? I'm catching up with people on Facebook that I literally last saw in the third grade, and it's fun. It's incredibly fun and cool, but it's also, "Am I really making a connection there? Am I trying to relive the past, which is always a mistake?" I mean, the past is the past for a reason, right? Okay, I knew these people in third grade, when we were eight years old. They've got families and mortgages and whatever now, as do I, and is there any relevance to our connecting now?

Is there any relevance to the characters in *Diary of the Dead* who might be around to watch the security video of the zombie attack when the guy gets supposedly electrocuted in the bathtub but then comes back? Is footage of any banal thing relevant to them in the post-zomboc world? It's an interesting concept to think about, and like I've said all through the podcast, the best horror movies—and certainly the best zombie movies—make us think about horrific or unsettling things in deeper and surprising ways.

FN: *Shaun of the Dead* addresses that I think is a very contemporary idea. As you've noted before, *Shaun* works as a straight-up zombie movie as well as a comedy, but there's also the resonant experience of Simon Pegg's character, Shaun. The zombie apocalypse is forcing him to understand what a waste of a human being he's been. At the start of the movie, he's that very typical alienated Gen-Xer who's not doing anything with his life. I think it really is a fear held by that crowd who made the Gen-X satire series *Spaced* with Pegg, Edgar Wright, and Nick Frost. This idea that, while he's afraid of the zombie apocalypse, he's also facing this anxiety he has about growing up and having to get a job and take care of himself in the world.

Hoade: I absolutely agree. *Shaun of the Dead* is one of everybody's favorite movies; it's one of my favorites, and one of the things that they do so brilliantly in that is that Shaun and his roommate, Ed, and the rest of them are living as zombies *even though they're alive.* One of the jokes in the beginning of the movie is you have a shot of these feet shambling and hear these moans, and it's like, "Oh no, a zombie!" But it's just Shaun yawning, getting up in the morning, living this repetitive life, this zombie-like existence. You see the check-out girls, with their eyes glazed over. They're doing the repetitive jobs and things like this, again and again, and so the observation is made that most of society's people are practically zombies already zombies, but it takes an *actual* zombie infestation to wake him up to life. When he is forced going to take his girlfriend to the Winchester, because he forgot to make the reservations at the nice restaurant, once again we see Dante's level of

Hell where people are doomed to forever make the same choices and same mistakes they made through life. That's almost the *definition* of a zombie.

So, in *Shaun of the Dead*, the fear is that we're all wasting our lives—in the First World we have the greatest technology, we have more knowledge than any time in history, we have the ability to keep our health at the very best anybody could have, and we—and I'm talking about myself also—we waste it. We don't use it for anything wonderful. We are zombies in our own lives, and I definitely think that in *Shaun of the Dead*, the part that wasn't meant to be horror-movie scary—that is, the movie before the zombies show up—actually was intensely scary because of how much it hit home, especially for this generation, the Gen-Xers. Now it's the millennial generation or Smartphone generation or whatever you want to call it—they see (or don't see) how their lives are being frittered away with this constant *American Idol*, *Survivor*, infotainment universe—it's just all a waste of time.

My wife, in fact, who of course is in charge, she will not allow me to get cable because she knows that I will enter complete zombiehood, alpha waves, sitting there watching a 30-hour marathon of some cooking or tattoo reality show. I'll be sitting there completely wasting my time, and with zombies it's so obvious that, "Oh my God, look at them, they're just wandering around, and if they see something that they want, they lurch after it, and then they forget about it and lurch at something else," but that's also describing us, the living. A terrible fear is the knowledge that if you were bitten by a zombie and turned into one of the undead yourself, except for the cannibalism you might not really be all that different from what you are now.

I think the banal nature of most people's lives—what Thoreau called "lives of quiet desperation"—you see a lot of people who seem *excited* by the idea of the zombies coming down and destroying civilization, by a nuclear war leaving us as Road Warriors or Wasteland Warlords. I can't say that I haven't been in this group occasionally, those who hope for some sort of apocalyptic situation, like a comet wiping almost everything out, or a zombie apocalypse starting, because then we have a challenge we can rise to! Those of us who are alive can rise to this challenge and fulfill the hero's quest. We were talking about *Cloverfield*, where the main character has an actual quest. The world has changed with extreme suddenness. He's not now going to go off to France or wherever it was and get this great job and all this stuff. He's going to go find the woman he loves and save her, and if she's dead, he'll know that and maybe he'll die with her, not let her enter the darkness alone. I mean, what could be more noble than that? These are the stories we read.

These are the fantasy experiences we want to have.

My wife and I went to see *Wicked,* and it's set *in Oz,* for God's sake, a completely unreal place, and yet it's through that, the realm of fantasy— and it's got witches, right, so you could even call it horror or whatever—that you can examine what is it to really be a friend, what is it to really be good or bad or wicked. In that impossible cauldron, what see what we really boil down to.

And that's why you see people saying, "I *hope* there's a zombocalypse, man, because then I can really show all these assholes what I'm made of." I think the fear is that life is more like the early part of *Shaun of the Dead* than when the zombies show up. We'll just keep going on and on, punching the clock and getting older and older, and our hair will get thinner, our asses will get fatter. And our kids are doomed to do the same worthless, unheroic life, which may be the ultimate horror. It's like, oh, Jimmy, do something with your life. Don't do what I did; that's what every parent says. I think that's the anxiety and why a lot of people—

FN: A lot of people, I think, feel like they don't have an opportunity to prove that they're great human beings because of the way things are set up today. Society gives advantages to people whose parents had advantages because *their* parents had advantages. I think some people wish that it all could be brought back to nature, and we could get a clean start.

Hoade: Right, more primal! Then the people who *do* have these societal advantages, what do they do with it? They get a nice car; they get the big house. In the end, it's frickin' J. Alfred Prufrock, where we get our trousers rolled and have our thinning hair and walk stooped over, and then that's it. We're dead without ever having really lived.

So for some, a zombocalypse or other apocalyptic scenario could be the best thing that could happen. It would certainly spice things up! We're talking about the horror genre of film, but when a girlfriend forces her boyfriend to go see *The Notebook*, and then she says, "Why can't *you* love me like that?" What can the guy say? "Um, well, get old and get Alzheimer's and I'll love you like that, I guess?" I mean, there's no way to win in a horror movie, or in a romantic drama. You want to have an exciting life, but you don't want the consequences.

Lesson 7
Zombies and Religion

FN: Today we're going to be wrapping up our FilmNerds guide to zombies with a look at the way that the undead have been used to analyze attitudes about religion and metaphysics.

In previous podcasts, we talked about how zombie fiction has touched on some contemporary fears, ideas that may have come to the fore only in the last ten years or so, but today we're going to look at some deeper, more ancient qualities built into us that zombie fiction also picks up on. That's religion, obviously something that's been a part of human civilization for a very long time. It's interesting that, as we record this, it's right around Easter time, which is of course when Christians celebrate the resurrection of their savior, and I think it's primarily this part of the zombie concept that really irks religious people, at least in the Western world, and sparks their religious fears and anxieties. The idea of life after death being a positive thing, being a beautiful thing, is really a huge appeal of religion for a lot of people, and obviously, zombie fiction turns this idea on its head, right, Sean?

Hoade: Yes, definitely. In all of my lectures and things when I talk about zombies, somebody always brings up, "Hey, Jesus was a zombie, right? You know, Jesus is the *ultimate* zombie! Easter is a zombie holiday!" I, because I like my job and want to keep it, try to steer clear of that. Jesus, it should be said—let's say that the Bible tales are true, and he was resurrected from the dead. Well, then he was *resurrected* from the dead. He was *no longer dead*. (And he wasn't undead, either, just alive again by the hand of God.) Zombies are definitely dead, and so Jesus, for the forty days after he came out of the tomb of Joseph of Arimathea, he wasn't rotting, he wasn't converting people via biting them, and he wasn't eating brains, so I think we can exempt Jesus from being a zombie. I think we can give him a pass on that.

FN: Undead doesn't mean you're not dead anymore. It means you are dead yet animate, isn't that correct?

Hoade: Right! "The ambulatory dead." Is that what we should call them?

FN: That would be the politically correct term if they existed today, I think.

Hoade: There could be the ACLU, the American Civil Liberties of the Undead—well, no, that acronym has been take [Laughs.] I teach a class on the apocalypse, and of course when you teach a class on the apocalypse, people always want to talk about zombies because that's the most fun kind of apocalypse, in part, I believe, because it's not actually possible. I don't want to disappoint your listeners, but I used this kind of a light, humorous book on the apocalypse, on all the different ways it could happen. I know sounds like, "How could there be a *light* book on that?"

But it was about how movies deal with the apocalypse and she treats the subject as if what movies did made sense—so it's pretty hilarious. Yet, despite all the zombie movies out there, she devotes just a single page to zombies because she feels that a zombocalypse is not really worth talking about as an apocalypse.

I was really surprised, you know? But then I read her explanation in that if a zombie apocalypse happened, if people rise from the dead, okay, not like a *28 Days Later...* disease thing, but people rise from the actual dead, well, then God is involved. God alone—according to our monotheistic religions—has the power to raise people from the dead. If they're going to be raised from the dead and be just alive again or if they're raised from the dead and be undead and have a taste for your brain, and thus they're going to destroy you, then that's the way God wants to wipe us out—not by fire or by water, but by zombie. It's up to God, right? And she said, if God decides that he's going to wipe you out, there's nothing you can do. I mean, you might get a pass by being especially noble and faithful, like Noah, being especially pure, but if

God decides that you, the human race, are going to die by zombie, then golly gee willikers, you're going to die by zombie, and there's really nothing to talk about.

It's *God*. There's no way we can prevent what God wants to do, even if in our opinion it's horrible, because God in the Judeo-Christian-Abrahamic tradition is all-powerful and all-knowing and all-good, so he thinks it's the right thing to do, he knows if you want to thwart his will, and he can easily stop you if you try. So really, to this person that was writing this book, there was really no point in discussing the zombocalypse because there's nothing anyone can do, there's nothing interesting to say. "Zombies! The End." Not much of a story, right?

FN: So she doesn't want to discuss any apocalyptic scenario brought about by an act of God, as I guess you would say?

Hoade: Right. I mean, by a theist god. I suppose a deist God would just sit back watch, but he would have set up a world where zombies could happen in the first place. Yes. I mean, you have your deist god who—you know, the Newtonian "sets everything in motion and then sits back and doesn't have any hand in what happens anymore" God. A deist god, if we get hit by a meteor and it wipes out the Earth, that's indirectly caused by God in that he set up the rules of nature and everything, but not in the way that a theist, interventionist God points his finger at the asteroid and moves it into a course where it will smash into Earth (or miss it, for that matter). So, that's the difference between the theist and the deist god for our purposes here. There's no way that an actively involved, interventionist God can be fought. There's no way that you, trying to end the zombie nightmare, can do anything about it, so let's just talk about the other ways the world can end. It was a reasoned and effective way to treat the subject in her book ... but I was a bit disappointed because I *always* want zombies to be a part of the picture. [Laughs.]

Still, it's an interesting dilemma for a religious person, because if such a person sees a zombie, or is witnessing a zombie infestation, he or she have two choices, right? There's "Well, God has decided that I am going to die by zombie and I am then probably going to become a zombie myself, which is a horrible way of being dead," right? Okay, not fun. Or that person can say that the devil has created this zombie pandemic, and now I must fight it on God's behalf! But either way, it's a supernatural thing, not like protecting the world from polio. If a meteor is heading for Earth, we can fire rockets at it or we can all just clap our hands and say, "Okay, everybody, let's get to the other side of the Earth real quick!"

FN: Get Ben Affleck in a space shuttle.

Hoade: Right? He will just—he'll *emote,* and that will scare the meteor off. [Laughs.]

Or you can say, "You know what? I'm *not* going to attribute this to God, who as I understand him is all-good. I'm going to fight this the best that I can. I don't know what the cause is—that God's catch: we can never know what he's thinking—but I'm going to fight it!" That is the most interesting, the most interesting way to look at a zombie infestation in terms of metaphysics. God would be have to be involved with a zombie apocalypse, even if he just allows it to happen. This is the zombocalypse if you think of it in terms of metaphysics, not just epidemiology or radiation or other scientific.

FN: I think one thing that bothers a lot of people and really becomes one of the more disturbing elements of the genre is that idea that death is supposed to work a certain way, according to the rules that I've been taught and the religious understanding that I believe I've gained. Death is supposed to go a certain way, at least in monotheistic religions: We die, and our souls go to some reward or punishment, and the body itself doesn't matter anymore since it no longer contains a soul or animating force. But then the zombie movie asks this terrible "what if" about the afterlife—maybe simply asking the question is the scary part—what if the afterlife isn't what

I think it's going to be at all, but instead will be a place of horror and pain because of a condition contracted here on Earth, something that isn't my fault at all?

Hoade: You go to your priest or your pastor or your rabbi or imam or whatever and ask, "What's the afterlife like?" They say, "If you're good or one of the elect, this happens; if you're bad, that happens. None of them look around real quick and then whisper, Actually, when you die, you might come back and eat people and do really evil things that you have no control over and also you're not the identity you know now. Say, have you heard about Freud's *uncanny?*" Your priest or spiritual adviser, whoever, wouldn't tell you this even if it *were* true because it's irrelevant to his or her mission: a zombie afterlife doesn't have much to say on being a good person versus being a bad person. You'll have to make choices just like in the rest of your life.

Vampires, on the other hand ... the stories are "If you become a vampire, your soul is damned. You're now the undead, the unholy. You can't enter consecrated ground," and all this stuff. This is why we really want to be careful not to fall under the spell of such a creature and do everything we can to prevent our loved ones from it as well. We really understand, even though it's a fictional concept, what it *means* metaphysically to become a vampire, but to become a zombie, in religious terms, what does it mean? Are you "damned"? Is your soul (should that be a real thing) even in there, is it even involved? I mean, if you do have a soul still in the reanimated body, are *you* then responsible for the evil acts that you're doing, munching on people? Are you now going to Hell?

FN: Sure, and one thing that's jumping to me that examined that a little bit—and I do mean just a little—is in *Day of the Dead*, there's some experimentation going on. The mad scientist gives a few lines of dialogue where he feels like he's starting to figure out how zombiism works, and I think one of the things he says is that only *part* of the self has been destroyed in the zombies. Basically, there is a part of the brain— and a part of the mind even, the personality— that's remains even after one is turned and undead. That's one example of a zombie film that says, "Well, maybe you're *not* all gone— maybe some of it is still you that is that zombie.

Hoade: That's one of the reasons that *Day of the Dead* is such a philosophically interesting movie. You've got Bub the Skinner-conditioned zombie, right? I mean, Bub, I love Bub. Bub remembers that he was in the military. He can remember what a book is for. He can't read, but he can pick the book up and look at it. He develops a bond with the doctor, and he realizes that Captain Rhodes is evil, and when he gets loose, he doesn't go on the rampage and start eating people. He is amused and goes to find the doctor and show him, hey, look, my chain came off the wall.

Then he sees that the doctor—his *friend*— has been murdered, and he puts it together that it was done by the evil Captain Rhodes, and then of course he ends up shooting Captain Rhodes and feeding him to the other zombies, and then there's his wonderful, sarcastic salute.

That asks the question, though: Is the self, made up of identity and memories and moral choices—is that identical with what we call "the soul"? Does that mean that where there's a self, there's a soul? No one in millennia of thought on this subject has been able to identify what the answer would be if you have two people who look exactly alike, act exactly alike, but one of them has a soul and the other hasn't—what is the detectible difference? Until we can identify even what it might be, we can't say anything about it from a reasoned standpoint.

FN: I think that's one part of the religious content of zombie films that particularly interests Christians: a belief that there's this duality happening throughout life between the body and the soul, and that we somehow have the ability for the soul to be master of the corporeal body, that who we *really* are is not completely connected to the body, that there can be some separation from that animalistic part of us. And obviously, what happens to you if you become a zombie, is you lose control over that. It's that fear of "What if I'm *not* able to master my body? What if my body will win that battle? Am I still *me?*"

Hoade: Kind of like when we talked about *Zombie Honeymoon,* this concept of the zombie corporeality becoming dominant—it has a certain resonance with how people deal with loved ones who are slowly (or quickly) being overtaken by a wasting or invasive disease. Are "they" still in there?

But a zombie film looked at in a slightly different way may actually offer a small comfort to the characters going through a zombie apocalypse or infestation of any size. Maybe what makes that person the person who loved definitely isn't there anymore. Let's say your mother gets bitten, and she of course succumbs to it and dies and is dead for thirty seconds or whatever and then comes back and is this flesh-eating monster. In this way of thinking, it *really isn't* your mother anymore. She's gone. Your mother's soul, if there is such a thing, has gone on to wherever souls go. Your mother, the *essence* of who she was, is not in that body.

This leads us to two conclusions: One, your mother isn't watching herself in horror as she attacks people she loves against her will; and two, your mother is exempted from responsibility for moral choices that her zombie body makes, because *it's not her inside there.* Her empty body has just become this artificially animated thing like a puppet on strings. Oh, and there's a third benefit of this kind of viewpoint: you don't have to feel bad about shooting this thing in the head, because it's not your mother. Have fun with it! [Laughs.]

Your mom died and that's terrible but was going to happen one day anyway. That's a separate issue of grief. But now you could take this zombie shell, put it on the rack, and do all sorts of horrible things to it, and mom's not going to feel anything because she's not there.

It's important to remember that, should there be a zombie pandemic and your mother (God forbid) is bitten and becomes a zombie, we can never know if her soul or identity or what have you really is, in actuality, in there or not. Remember, we can't say for sure if a soul is present because we don't even know what a soul actually *is*, even theoretically.

One plus if there ever were an actual zombie crisis is, like in World War II with all of the scientific leaps forward, I bet you there would be a lot of work on what a soul is and an official answer, with scientific explanations provided. It would be like the Manhattan Project of metaphysics.

It would suddenly change from "That's intellectually and/or theologically interesting" to "We *need* to know if there's a person in there or not." So theologically, it is fascinating, but the

Spanish zombie movie series of the early '70s, *Tombs of the Blind Dead*—expressed the very big-C Catholic idea that one's body is really nothing but a vehicle for the soul. The body itself is stained and unclean in ways that the soul never really could be, because it is on loan from God. You might do bad things, but you can always seek forgiveness and your soul can be cleansed, saved—this is the Catholic idea specifically, but true of many Christian denominations. But your body—that's just a container.

Your soul can be cleansed, but your body, if you lose an arm, you're not going to grow your arm back because there's no *real* importance to it in the long run. If you're dead—you're not going to come back from the dead usually—but the Catholic idea is that the body without a soul is like feces, just the waste product of existence with no religious importance. This concept makes the zombie even fouler than it would be otherwise because not only is it an abomination because it kills, but even more it's an abomination because it has no connection whatsoever to God. I think that, to the Spanish Catholics who made and watched this movie, was an uniquely horrifying idea.

FN: Sure, yes. As I said, I think I may have attributed that to all Christians, but personally I'm Catholic, I was raised Catholic, and I think that's something that does permeate into us from Catholic doctrine in the way that we approach things. There is that idea that there's, like I said, a duality, a very strict difference between your body and your soul, and your body isn't really looked upon as your true *self* at all.

You are something other than that, and your body is simply a vehicle, your way to be here on Earth, and it's your responsibility to control it and make sure that you don't do evil things with it. And I think it's part of that unconscious fear there: "What if I had absolutely no control over my body, whether I was there or not?" And the zombie is the idea of the body run amok with no immortal soul there to keep it in check.

Hoade: Not only no guiding intelligence, but no connection to God whatsoever, and some people say—I mean, I believe this is the Catholic doctrine—that this is what purgatory is. I could completely have this wrong, but isn't purgatory is a place where people don't have the punishment of hell, they're not being actively punished, but their suffering comes from their having no further access to God.

FN: Sure. It's the purification time that you must go through to get to heaven. It's definitely not seen as a good place to be: you don't want to be there, because, like you said, your connection to the Divine is severed. You don't have the illusions of the physical world to keep you occupied and allowing you not to think about it. You're completely aware now that there's an afterlife and that there is a God, but you are completely cut off from him.

Hoade: And that's the worst, to know there's a God and be severed from God! But that seems to be exactly what the zombie existence is according to Catholicism. Why the Italian and Spanish filmmakers of the '70s were able to use that so effectively was because there Catholicism is very dominant in those countries, and so it's a fear that everybody in those audiences was in touch with, that everybody shared. "I don't want to go where I can't be in touch with God because of a zombie!" Also, it's like, "Why does my body want me to commit this sin? *I* don't want it!"

Which of course has a lot to do with actual Catholic experience, that spiritual and mental war against sinful bodily desires. Why does my body want me to have an adulterous relationship or steal or commit other sins? It's always, "I want to steal this food so I can eat it" or "I must kill this man because he slept with my wife and I am angry." There are reasons that the body demands these things, even if they are terrible reasons, and that's why the soul part of a person can be forgiven.

But a zombie? It commits the most vile of sins without any justification or reasoning at all. Being a zombie is just the lowest state religiously, and I don't think just with Catholicism. In any kind of religion, a body without a soul is unclean in that spiritual way, but also it's a state that no one would want to be in. If that doesn't sum up zombiehood, I don't know what does.

FN: One other zombie connection to religious ideas is that part of what makes everything go so wrong during a zombie apocalypse is, as human beings, we want to be heroes. It's part of our natural inclination, especially among men, whether this is something evolved or whether this is religiously a trait that's a part of us being made in the image of God, who is seen as the ultimate hero.

We want to save the people whom we love, and *that* in these zombie films is so often what causes more bad things to happen. Like you said in an earlier episode, if everyone just tried to save themselves, the zombie apocalypse wouldn't spread as quickly, but I think that really goes against the Christian idea of the Messiah who saves everyone by sacrificing himself—that's something that has seeped into fiction in the Western world very, very extensively. I mean, you can point to many, many films—not just zombie movies—that don't appear to have any other religious implications, but you can point to the hero of those films and say, well, that's coming from the idea of Jesus sacrificing himself to save everyone else.

Hoade: Good point. I mean, this is true even movies like *Sin City*. It has the word "sin" in the title, for goodness' sake. You have the Mickey Rourke and also the Bruce Willis character, who sacrifice themselves to save the girl. They're anti-heroes, sure, but they're still heroes because they sacrifice themselves for something pure, something that they feel is purer than themselves or more worthy. They become heroes.

I mean, the Christ model has essentially *defined* "hero" in Western literature, or at least serves one of the main models. Certainly, I think, if you look at a lot of these zombie films, that character either doesn't exist at all, or doesn't use his sacrifice to triumph in the way we expect heroic characters to. There is rarely a zombie film where someone has an opportunity to sacrifice themselves to save everyone else, and then they do it, and it works.

In fact, I can't think of *any* zombie movie in the Romero era where that happens. You do see, certainly, some sacrificial heroes, but it's more done pyrrhically to show love for one particular person. It certainly doesn't stave off the zombies for long, and then most of the time we see that the heroes who ultimately win in the zombie movies are the ones who look out for themselves rather than the ones who give themselves up to save the other people.

Thus is created the theological and philosophical question: Have these selfish people, people who have triumphed over being eaten by zombies, *really* won anything important?

I mean no, they haven't been killed by the zombies. And no, they haven't died in some heroic way like the security guard in the van at the end of the *Dawn of the Dead* remake where he takes a whole bunch of zombies out—and also kills himself—by shooting the propane tank. He did that so his death would not be in vain. But they haven't "won" just by surviving, at least not in the eyes of most religions.

If you win by ignoring the cries and needs of others, of what value is that victory? You have not won in the way that our society and our religions and even our human nature would consider winning. If I cheat in a race and I win, well, I still technically get the trophy, but it's not the same morally as if I had *really* won. So, in a zombie movie, if I get away myself, I get away in my helicopter, but I leave these other people behind because there I didn't want to risk having a zombie get in, it's a meaningless victory in the eyes of the audience and of God. Your life from then on is but half a life, and metaphysically you have condemned yourself to something worse than death.

We've mentioned many things about zombie films in these podcasts that are scary and unsettling, from the idea of the uncanny to the fear of contagion to the mechanics of survival in an undead world. But one of the most haunting aspects of zombie stories is that right and wrong are turned upside-down. If we sacrifice ourselves by jumping between the zombie horde and our friends, we will soon be a zombie ourselves and directly increase the danger the survivors will face.

"I'll hold off these zombies while you get in the car and get away!" Okay, great, but then you're part of the menace, so have you won? Have you really helped protect them? Are you a hero? Maybe for the moment, but not in any kind of long-term, meaningful way. And zombies, of course, aren't sacrificing themselves.

FN: They're the ultimate "I'm out for number one" type.

Hoade: Precisely. They don't even really notice the other zombies. (Except in *Land of the Dead,* a weird departure for Romero which even he didn't repeat.) As soon as somebody is turned into a zombie, the other undead are like, huh, he's not food anymore, I'm not interested in him.

One of the great examples of that is in the original *Dawn of the Dead,* when Flyboy is on the elevator. He's been bitten, and he gets in the elevator, and he's dying, and all the zombies are trying to get in the elevator because he's still alive in there, so they can get him; but when the doors open and he's a zombie, they literally all turn away in complete disinterest.

FN: I'm sure you have a much wider experience with zombie fiction than most of us have, and I wonder, in terms of outside the Christian world or at least outside Europe and the United States, are there zombie films and zombie stories from Asia or other parts of the world that take a different approach to the genre based on the religious ideas that come from those parts of the world, like Hinduism or Buddhism?

Hoade: Well, that's an interesting question, because in Southeast Asia—South Korea, Thailand, Singapore—there was a lot of fear over the SARS epidemic. This led directly—as societal fears always do—into the creation of zombie films. There's *Bio-Zombie*, there's one called *SARS Wars*, and they weren't badly done. Some of them were more slapsticky and humorous and others more serious, but they were playing with ideas cobbled from American zombie films. The characters get stuck in a mall, or there's a chemical spill bringing back the dead, or something like that.

Fighting zombies in films made in Buddhist countries creates an interesting dilemma. In Zen and just about every other sect of Buddhism, you are just supposed to go with the flow of basically whatever happens. You should be harmless and strong. You shouldn't even kill a zombie because they appear to be sentient creatures. They seem sentient because they can react to the world around them, kind of like a bug. A bee doesn't want to sting you, but that's its nature—that's what it will do if it feels a certain stimulus. You shouldn't even kill a bee because you then interfere with its karmic journey. So in Buddhism, killing is the worst thing you can do, karmically speaking. It's all based on karma. The questions then become— and there's no Pope of Buddhism, so I don't know who would answer it—"Is putting down a zombie actually killing, since it's already dead? Are they sentient beings or not? Is *wanting* to kill a zombie against what the Buddha taught?" These, to me, are fascinating conundrums.

Then you have the idea of the zombie in Islam, which is really interesting because anything that happens is the express will of Allah. (This is why terrorists are condemned by most of the Islamic world: the terrorists are fighting against the way Allah has created things.) So it's an alien idea, this "Why would God allow this to happen?" or "Is this part of His plan? Why was this bad person spared, and I wasn't?" I'm sure individual Muslims have questions, but strictly speaking, in Islam, whatever happens is the will of Allah, and that's just how it is, zombies included. To say that zombies are bad is to say that Allah made a bad decision, which is literally meaningless in Islam.

It's completely theistic and completely fatalistic, at least on paper. It doesn't really matter if the zombie bites me or not because I've been a good Muslim and I'm going to go to Heaven, or I've been a bad Muslim and I'm going to go to hell. It doesn't really matter what happens with the zombie because if it bites me, Allah has willed it. If I'm able to fight it off, Allah has willed that. I really am just a supplicant to Allah.

Two caveats here: One, I'm sure the reality of a zombie infestation would induce more immediately practical efforts to stave off an apocalypse. And two, I haven't seen any Islamic zombie movies, so I don't know what their treatment would be. But I'd love to see one!

Hoade: There have definitely been a lot of Thai zombie flicks, and Thailand has a large—but minority—Muslim population. The zombie films from Thailand have tended to be either more Buddhist in flavor or not incorporating religion at all. I don't even know what a Muslim zombie movie would look like. There really isn't a lot to say if you're just going, "Oh, well, it's Allah's will." There's not much of a story there. The characters would have no motivation—or if they did, they could be seen as taking action that is meant to be against the will of Allah. Kind of a no-win situation there for Islamic zombie cinema.

FN: It almost frees you up to tell the story in a way, because if it's going to happen, I guess it's as good as any other story.

Hoade: If all stories are equal, then which are worth telling? Some stories say that the Muslims burned the library at Alexandria and said about the many books: "If it's got something that's *not* in the Koran, it's blasphemous; and if it's something that *is* in the Koran, it's redundant. So burn them all."

This isn't to be anti-Muslim at all. I'm just saying, as far as storytelling goes, I don't know if an Islamic zombie movie would be interesting. But who knows? Maybe next month they will come out with one! But the Buddhist-influenced ones are really interesting, because how can you fight zombies while also swearing to do no harm?

FN: So zombies are another stop on the wheel of life to Buddhists?

Hoade: Well, they are. In fact, zombies very closely represent—or resemble—a stage in the cosmology of Buddhism called the *preta,* or "hungry ghost." The hungry ghost has a very small mouth and a very large stomach, so it's always really hungry. It just lives in this constant state of terrible hunger. It's incapable of having compassion because can only think of the craving for food. It is able only to watch out for itself. Even within that horrible state, however, there are certain things that can show a little bit of compassion or a little bit of not harming others that gives a *preta* enough good karma to move on to the next level, which is the animal realm.

FN: So it wouldn't be a good thing to destroy one of those beings because we're all going to be there someday, possibly?

Hoade: Exactly. In fact, according to Buddhist cosmology, we've all been there countless times and unless we get liberated, will be there countless times to come. We've gone up and down the ladder of life—or gone around the wheel of life—but the thing is that if there really is such an entity as a hungry ghost, then it's really to be pitied, not to be destroyed, and that makes fighting zombies really tough. That tension is that's one of the things that makes Buddhist-themed zombie stories interesting. In Christianity, there are arguments in support of such a thing as "righteous killing," but in Buddhism there really aren't. (Although S.T. Suzuki perverted Zen through Japanese nationalism during World War II to induce men to fight and die. That said, we've all done bad things. It's just more trips to the lower realms of existence for us to endure.)

FN: So it becomes that much harder for characters in Buddhist zombie movies to do what they need to in order to survive?

Hoade: Well, I think it starts out mostly with, you have a character who is a good Buddhist and doesn't want to harm others. Usually that character gets eaten fairly early on, and then you have pretty much standard Hollywood-type zombie movies. Most of them are "Buddhist" zombie movies in that they use the cultural tropes of Buddhism, but end up usually being people fighting the undead like usual.

But at least these movies make a nod toward Eastern religion. It's like in *Dawn of the Dead.* "When hell is full, the dead will walk the Earth." There's your nod to Christianity. It's a concession that anything dealing with life and death, by definition, is a metaphysical question.

I don't know if I've ever seen a zombie movie using Hindu themes.

FN: Yes, I was wondering if there have maybe been any Bollywood zombie films.

Hoade: No, not that I've seen. But that could be really cool.

FN: There'd have to be a dance number.

Hoade: Wouldn't that be great? It would be like "Thriller" all over again, but with more bling.

FN: Well, Sean, this has been just a fascinating series. I just want to say again how much I appreciate having you on for these FilmNerd podcasts. Thanks again for joining us.

Hoade: Well, I want to thank you, too, though, for treating—this may sound silly—but for treating the zombie genre with the respect that it really deserves. The zombie idea itself is a little bit silly, but what's not silly at all is how we as humans have created and developed this myth, especially over the past hundred years. It really speaks volumes about where we are in civilization and in the world and in our religious thinking and in our moral thinking, so I think this podcast is going to go a long way toward convincing people that it is actually something worthy of talking about.

FN: We joke about us being "film nerds" because it's a nerdy thing to do in the eyes of many, to take something like zombie movies seriously, but all of us who have worked on these podcasts believe that we can learn a lot from our pop culture. And I think zombie fiction is a perfect example of that. We've talked through this series about some really interesting issues, the kinds of things that intellectuals in any hall at any university in the world would talk about. We've just used zombie movies as our jumping-off point.

Hoade: This really has been an online master's degree in Zombie Studies, hasn't it? [Laughs.]

Professor Zombie's Clip File

A collection of articles from around the world featuring your favorite zombie expert explaining the myths, the legends, and the realities surrounding the living dead.

WHITE ZOMBIE

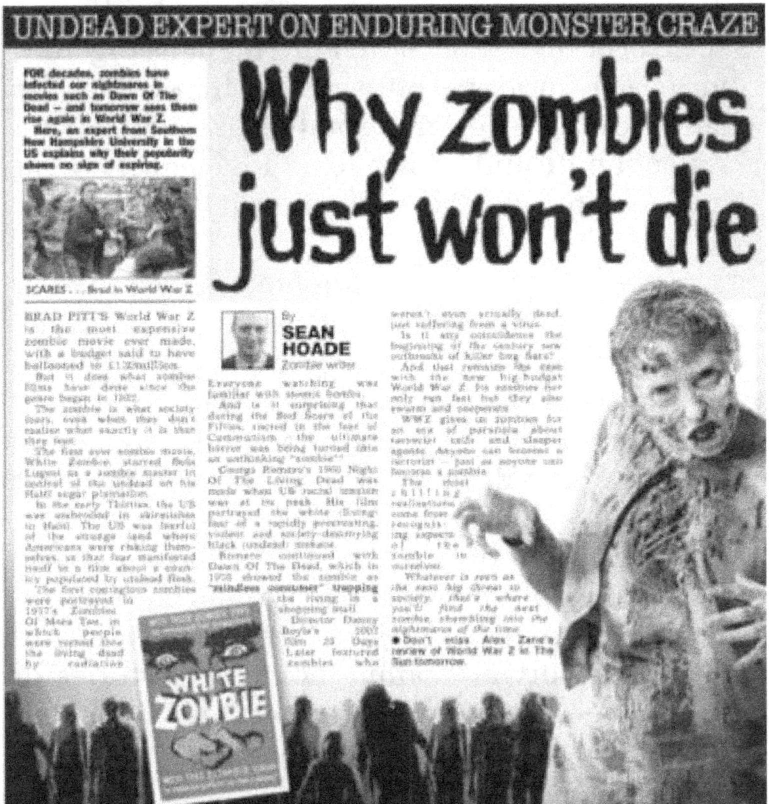

(Below is the full text of my *Sun* essay. Above is the cool layout they used for it in the print version of the paper.)

The zombie is what society fears.

Brad Pitt's *World War Z,* which opens this week as the most expensive zombie movie ever made, may feature a type of undead menace that's brand-new to the genre—socially cooperative revenants, able to make bridges to scale over high walls or to herd humans together for easier hunting—but the new film is just the latest example of the zombie as a cinematic reflection of underlying fears in a society, as it has been during every era since its inception in 1932.

Take that first zombie movie, *White Zombie,* starring Bela Lugosi as a sorcerous zombie master, in control of legions of the undead who work on his sugar plantation until they are crushed in machinery or dispatched by the taste of salt (yes, salt) or falls from great heights.

At the time of that American film, the early 1930s, the U.S. was embroiled in skirmishes and protection activity in Haiti, with many of the men then serving coming home with stories of (as William Seabrook put it in his 1928 book that inspired the movie) "dead men working in the cane fields."

The fears expressed in that first zombie movie were threefold: First, the U.S. was fearful of the strange land in Haiti where Americans were risking themselves, so that fear made (undead) flesh was horrifying.

Second, the United States was still a hotly racist society in many places, and the story of a white woman (the "white zombie" of the title) being made into a creature that consorted with Haitian Black men struck a chord not just among bigots but also among people imagining themselves more enlightened but who feared the "Black menace" subconsciously.

And finally, Haiti became a home for the ancestors of Black residents now because they were brought their as slaves to harvest sugar cane, freedom from toil coming only at their deaths. Imagine, then, the horror of being made to work forever as an undead slave, creatures not sharing the island nation's unshackling from France in 1804.

The zombie is what society fears, even when they don't realize what it is exactly that they fear.

But the zombies of modern times aren't voodoo zombies with a master controlling them—in fact, part of their skin-crawling appeal is that NOTHING controls them, other than their insatiable hunger. That is terrifying, and so is the idea that a person can be "infected" by a zombie and become one him- or herself!

The first contagious zombies were portrayed in 1957's *The Zombies of Mora Tau*, in which people were made into zombies by radiation, and as everyone during that period knew from atomic bomb preparation, coming into contact with something radioactive makes YOU radioactive. And is it surprising that during the Red Scare of the late '50s, the ultimate horror was being turned in an unthinking, dangerous "zombie"? The Communists were trying to infect individual-minded Americans in the exact same way!

In 1968, however, George Romero's *Night of the Living Dead* changed the popular conception of a zombie forever. No magic was involved here (possibly technology in the form of a space probe returning from Venus), no radiation. In this film, anyone who died during that last day came back to life, insatiably hungry for human flesh. This was the beginning of the zombie as cannibal that we know so well today … but it was much more than that.

Romero's genius was in having the cannibalism on the living, possibly humanity's most unbreakable taboo, be the agent that infected the victim and made him or her into a zombie—who then feasted upon living humans and continued the cycle. It was completely new, completely disgusting and horrifying on both a visceral and an existential level. He continued and refined this idea through five more *Dead* films.

That was Romero's genius, but his luck was that the film was made at a time when racial tension was at its very highest in the U.S., and his film portrayed the White (living) fear of a rapidly procreating, violent, and society-destroying Black (undead) menace. The real stroke of luck, however, was when the filmmakers noticed that the best actor among them to play the lead was Duane Jones ... who was as middle-class-looking as he was African-American. It turned everything in *Night* inside-out and the racial undertones made into a fascinating Möbius strip of paranoia, irony, and disgust.

Romero continued with *Dawn of the Dead*, which, coming out in 1978, posited the zombie as "mindless consumer" trapping the living in a shopping mall—where the survivors turned into mindless consumers of a different kind. It was social comment of the highest order in the very lowest-brow form of entertainment, the monster movie.

Later *Dead* movies took on the militarism of the Reagan/Thatcher years, gated communities, and social media, always using the zombie as, on one level, an incisive commentary and on another as a gross-out monster perfect for the drive-in cinema.

By then, Romero's way of doing things caught on with other filmmakers, who found they didn't have to reinvent the wheel every time and could just use the concept of the "Romero zombie" of whom everyone knew the rules: slow, shambling, cannibalistic, dead.

But as modern life sped up, so did its undead; in fact, 2002's *28 Days Later* ... featured zombies who could run FAST and weren't even actually dead, just suffering from a virus that made them bite and infect others. In 2004's remake of "Dawn of the Dead," the zombies were again dead but now ran with almost superhuman speed.

Is it any coincidence that the beginning of the century saw SARS outbreaks and other contagions that required many people packed together in large cities in order to spread? Or that more than ever in the 2000s, on many people's minds is the end of days, brought on by disease or nuclear war or Judgment Day or even something as banal but deadly as the water running out? Again, the zombie is what society fears.

And that remains the case with the new and big-budget *World War Z*. The movie gets its title from Max Brooks's brilliant "oral history of the zombie war," but in the book the walking dead are 100 percent Romero zombies—while in the new movie, they are nothing the zombie movie has done before.

In *WWZ* the zombies are nice and undead, but now they not only run fast but they also swarm and cooperate like colonies of ants or bees, making structures with their body and herding prey in a way that benefits the superorganism. This is very much like social insects, where an individual seems purposeless and lost, but the more of them there are, the more emergent their behavior towards a goal.

But glamorous movie stars and $150 million dollar budget or no, a zombie movie portrays what society fears, and *WWZ* gives us zombies for an era of paranoia about terrorist cells and sleeper agents, when the enemy we fear works in concert with others, none of them capable of much damage by themselves but hugely dangerous the more of them there are.

It's no accident in the new movie's trailers that zombies take down airliners and destroy buses full of people—that's what terrorists create terror by doing. And anyone with exposure to the right combination of people and situation can become a terrorist, just as anyone can become a zombie. You can't tell by looking at them if it's your friend or just someone who is now turned against you.

World War Z is far from the first and won't be the last movie to show us what frightens us most by wrapping it in an exciting and traditionally scary cinematic experience. Whatever is perceived as the next big, scary threat to society, that's where you'll find the zombie, shambling into the nightmares of the time.

Zombies A to Z

By SARA STEWART

There are slow zombies, and there are fast zombies. But moviegoers may never have seen the likes of the latest breed of the undead, coming at you in *World War Z* on Friday: the swarming zombie.

In the Brad Pitt-produced adaptation of Max Brooks' best selling novel, Pitt plays Gerry, an ex-United Nations investigator and family man who finds his world upended when an epidemic begins turning people into the walking—and running and massing—dead.

"When they are not provoked, they are stagnant, slow and wandering," says the film's director, Marc Forster (*Quantum of Solace*). "When the feeding frenzy starts, it's almost like a shark that smells blood. In the moment they sense that there's something to attack, they will just go for it. It's the way flocks of birds or fish or ants move together. There is almost a 'swarm intelligence' to it."

It's the latest—and possibly most terrifying—development in the zombie genre, which has enjoyed a surging renaissance over the past decade. The zombie has never been so front-and-center in the public consciousness, which the director says is no accident.

"People are tied to their screens and their monitors and their headphones—in the most basic sense, they do walk around like zombies by not interacting with other human beings," he says. "Also, at least for me, the world feels like a tenuous place—it feels unstable. It feels like there are big waves of emotion and behavior that are sweeping over us, and it's happening more and more quickly."

But the idea of zombies as embodiments of our cultural unease is far from new. It dates back to 1932 and the release of a Bela Lugosi film, *White Zombie,* featuring a witch doctor who turns a young woman into a zombie slave. A decade later, we saw a more classic rendition of a zombie: the voodoo-induced state of the island native Carre Four in 1943's *I Walked With a Zombie.*

"The genre started with old Haitian folklore," says Peter Dendle, author of*The Zombie Movie Encyclopedia,* now out in Vol. 2. "During the US Marine occupation of Haiti, Marines brought back travel accounts—largely made up—of cannibalism and voodoo. Hollywood turned it into an icon of entertainment.

"The early years focus on appropriation of female bodies," Dendle adds. "The voodoo master would be abe to take over a woman's body and control her like a puppet."

Zombies also corresponded with a domestic concern: the Great Depression. "It did resonate with the images of soup lines made up of people whose souls were dug out, whose eyes were dead," says Dendle. "It was a population that had been gutted from within."

(My part starts here!—SH)

Then in the 1950s, "you had your first contagious zombies," says Sean Hoade, a writer and academic who created a seven-part iTunes series called *Zombies! The Living Dead in Literature, Film and Culture.*

"The zombies were radioactive," he says of 1957's *Zombies of Mora Tau.* "It was the start of the Cold War. Not a great film, but a milestone in zombie movies."

The film that put the undead on the map came in 1968: George Romero's *Night of the Living Dead,* which introduced the classic "shambling zombie," slow-moving but relentless, and still the mainstay of much zombie pop culture, as in TV's current smash, *The Walking Dead*.

Romero's plot reflected the nation's civil rights turbulence. "When you look at it as a racial element, it's this idea of 'look at the rapidly spreading people beneath us coming to ruin the elite,' " says Hoade, who adds that Romero threw in a twist: "Ben [the hero] is black. He wasn't written as black, but Duane Jones was the best actor among their friends, so he got the part."

Romero's subsequent *Dawn of the Dead* (1978) turned its focus to commercialism, setting the action in a shopping mall, while 1985's *Day of the Dead* pushed the envelope with a sentient zombie named Bub, who's captured and held at an underground Army base. "Bub the zombie speaks the only dialogue of any zombie in any of those films," says Hoade. "That's the first inkling there's intelligence there."

Bub was trained to follow orders, but "what they used as a reward was human flesh," Hoade points out. "We don't want that kind of conditioning!"

Fast zombies—or "zoombies," as Dendle calls them—made everything exponentially scarier when they arrived, first in Danny Boyle's *28 Days Later...* in 2002 and then in Zack Snyder's 2004 *Dawn of the Dead* remake. In *28 Days*, Cillian Murphy wakes to find himself in a London decimated by a "rage" virus that turns victims into ferocious, unstoppable monsters.

Boyle's film marked "the rebirth of the zombie genre," says Ross Payton, author of *Zombies of the World: A Field Guide to the Undead.* "You have a respected director, a great script, and you have a new type of zombie: the fast-running zombie."

28 Days played into our newly developing anxiety about pandemics, overpopulation and the vulnerability of our infrastructure.

"[Both films are] very much a comment on how we're all packed together, and a fear of epidemics in general," says Hoade. "Can you trust your neighbor? Are you prepared for systems to go down?"

It also mainstreamed zombie culture in a new way. "This last decade has been the most vital and creative and important in the genre's history," says Dendle. Also the most disturbing, with increasingly realistic effects giving the undead a believability they previously lacked.

"*The Walking Dead* has the best zombie effects of any movie or TV show, anything, ever," says Hoade. "They're brilliant.

"But," he laments, "that makes the completely inept storytelling that much sadder!"

Still, this soap-opera-fication normalized the zombie for millions of viewers, who tune in to AMC to watch Deputy Rick and company fight their way through the blighted landscape, picking off expertly styled zombies who looked eerily real.

The undead then grew a heart in *Warm Bodies*, earlier this year, in which Nicholas Hoult's zombie still had memories, feelings and the capacity to fall head over heels in love—with a human.

"I guess that was inevitable because of *Twilight*," says Payton. "But also it's getting into the trend of humanizing zombies. Pop culture is aware of the 'othering' of groups of people, and some people get uncomfortable with the idea of killing zombies—aren't they just people infected with a disease?"

But don't expect gooshy sentiments in the latest chapter in the zombie evolution. *World War Z*, from early accounts, is a harder-edged look at a world under siege from a zombifying epidemic. It veers sharply from its source material (which is subtitled "An Oral History of the Zombie War") to become a more traditional thriller in which Pitt's character is at the center of an unraveling world.

Though the studio has been cagey about showing the zombies in its film (or showing the film to press), those who have seen it say its zombies are at odds with the classic shambling breed in the book.

"In the movie," says Hoade, "what we have are super-fast zombies who can jump higher, run faster, which has nothing to do with the zombies in the book."

They also work in concert: "You see them making human bridges, hunting together to flush out prey," he says. "The mechanism for them to communicate, I'm sure, is that it's in the virus."

Picking up the baton from *The Walking Dead*, costume designer Mayes Rubeo went for super-realism in her depiction of the virus' ravages on the various zombies.

"We wanted to show the process from human to zombie through the costumes," she says. "Not everyone has the same bite, not everybody is hurt or traumatized in the same way. Every [zombie] has a specific design, including the aging of the wardrobe, the condition of the clothes, the amount of blood. We wanted to portray each one as an individual in a certain stage of the epidemic."

As for their movements, the designers cite a host of influences, from insects to the Coen brothers.

"We thought of movies that perhaps had a character without any humanity. We thought that Javier Bardem's character in *No Country for Old Men* had an interesting feel. We spent a lot of time trying to re-create what it might feel like to be him, so the movement came from within," says Ryen Perkins-Gangnes, the film's zombie movement ace.

"[We] also brought in images of insects feeding, how rapacious and relentless they are and their pace, which can go from really fast to slow and rhythmical and really fast again—this sort of insect-y, jaw-driven creature devoid of any humanity or sense of future or past, just stuck in the present moment."

Which might sound familiar to anyone who's lost three hours of a day to Facebook. Hoade says he sees a social-media angle in the film: "We now have the idea that we have all these 'friends' out there, but we don't really know them. And the idea that you know them but you don't really know them becomes literal in zombie movies."

Payton sees an element of the survivalist classic here. "There isn't that much wilderness anymore," he points out. "Everyone has cellphones. We have search and rescue. It's really hard to get lost. But if you want to do a man versus nature story, zombies are a great way of explaining why there's no one—without the unpleasant effects of something like a nuclear winter. It's a 'cozy catastrophe.' And you don't have to have a lot of backstory."

After all, he points out, these days "everyone knows what a zombie apocalypse is."

Zombie Nation

Zombie Walks are a recent street culture phenomenon. Karina Wilson explores their gruesome appeal.

Strange things are afoot in the malls, campuses and city streets of North America. Shambling, groaning things. with peeling skin and tattered clothes. Lurching, moaning things, with missing limbs and a thirst for 'braiiins'. They appear out of nowhere and vanish just as suddenly. They lack identity, but stand out in any crowd: Zombies. Hundreds of them.

This is not the long-dreaded apocalypse, however. It's not even TV news. Instead of grabbing the nearest shotgun and blowing off the ghouls' heads, citizens reach straight for their camera phones. And smile. The stumbling undead, far from inspiring screeching terror, are greeted with giggles. Shuffling corpses are the polar opposite of the plastic-perfect uber-beings splattered across the pages of celebrity magazines. They're stupid, ugly, and stink, but it seems we love us some ghoul-on-ghoul like never before. Welcome to the Zombie Nation.

In terms of popular culture, zombies are at the top of their game. They're the coolest currency imaginable in Hollywood, with Brad Pitt and Leonardo DiCaprio fighting a bidding war over the rights to *World War Z* before it was even published (Pitt's Plan B production company won). But cinema zombies are not enough for 20- and 30-something Americans, raised on the interactivity of gaming. They don't just want to watch them onscreen. They want to be them.

Traditionally, this is not something sane humans have desired. Your average zombie, whether the victim of a voodoo curse or an alien virus, is trapped in a transitory phase between life and death. They can't speak. Bits keep falling off. He/she is simply waiting for a well-aimed bullet to the head to end the misery. So, why the current enchantment with the living dead? Aren't zombies meant to be the cannibal plague, harbingers of terror, soul-less shells hell-bent on death and destruction? How did they get to be poster children for the Wii generation?

Dorm Of The Dead

Blame it on the Zeitgeist. Sean Hoade is an Instructor of English at the University of Alabama in Tuscaloosa, where he teaches a class titled *Zombies! The Living Dead in Literature,*

Film and Culture. He thinks "American" and "Zombie" make a good match.

"Zombies are creatures without a past," he says. "So, as a group, are Americans. Zombies want to consume, but don't really *need* what they consume (since their bodies don't require nutrition). This is the same with many Americans: We want to buy and consume, but our McMansions are filled to overflowing with things we never use. Also, zombies are largely ignorant of—even completely uninterested in— their fellow zombies. Well, what is America but the ultimate place where neighbors never even learn one another's names?"

He suggests zombies "act as a mirror for Americans, not only as we see ourselves but also as the rest of the world sees America in the time of George W. Bush: as a roaming, voracious killer turning its victims into soulless creatures like itself."

His students have embraced the idea of zombie studies. "Their eyes lit up and many of them said…"I love zombies! They're so cool!"" Hoade is bemused. "Now, why would intelligent young people, in the prime of their health and beauty, find "cool" a bunch of rotting dead bodies which happen to walk, bodies which have no personality, intelligence, or anything else one would look for in a friend or mate? I think it's because in our Western society, we're never really around death—the whole thing is utterly sanitized compared to even fifty years ago—and the zombie concept lets them "interact," if you will, with the concept and the physical reality of death, but without being overly morbid or depressing."

The Munch Bunch

It's not just in Alabama that playing dead seems like the coolest way to spend your weekend. And it's easier—and less of a permanent decision—than you might think to become part of the post-mortem ambulatory horde. From Baltimore to Texas, groups of like-minded individuals are organizing themselves into a specific form of flash mob—or flesh mob—via MySpace and FaceBook. Scan through the forums on www.zombiewalk.com and you'll find eager discussions about upcoming and recent zombie walks in most major cities across the US. And it seems other continents are fast latching on to the idea, with zombie walks organized in Australia, Canada and the UK.

Participants "cadaver up"—the real enthusiasts spending hours with layers of liquid latex and prosthetic limbs, while others simply tear some old clothes and sploosh themselves with fake blood—and then stumble through the streets of their home city in a loose, but instantly recognizable group. It's fun. It's very simple.

And it's seen by the 'stumblers' as a cheap and harmless way to get some kicks.

Will Jayne is part of a Saturday night stroll along Hollywood Blvd's Walk of Fame. "A bunch of people dressing up, scaring the crap out of strangers sounded like a great idea to me. I'm actually here with my girlfriend. We don't just want to sit at home and eat popcorn and scare ourselves, we want to go out there and be part of the action."

Fellow stumbler Erin Sirpinksi came because "it's really fun to play around and dress up. Some people will think this is a normal Saturday night in Hollywood—that's also fun because they're asking 'Are are they doing something? Is this organized or are they dressed like that cos they're Goth kids?' It's really fun to be able to congregate as a group and just do this...That's why I do it, for the fun."

For costume designer Crystal Wilkinson, walking with zombies is part of a wider set of choices. "I'm here because I have a fascination with occult fantasy, it's always been something that I've been into, ever since I was a little kid." It's not just an opportunity to dress up. Social comment is involved, however subtle it might be. "I think this is what American culture is. Everyone following other people, a mindless, brainless society, no one stepping outside of the box, no one doing anything to differentiate themselves from another person. Group society in general—I'm kind of against that. I'm all about individualism."

Sadly, even zombies have to play by society's rules. LAPD's finest also turn up to the Hollywood walk, summoned, not by some terrified citizen in fear of their brains, but by the maintenance staff at the Metro (LA's Underground) station who are, understandably, upset about the fake blood spilled on their usually-spotless floors by stumblers. The zombie horde are extremely apologetic about the mess, but offers to help clean up get rebuffed. Something about union rules.

The cops hang out for a bit, however, intrigued by the well behaved and sweet smelling undead, a far cry from the usual homeless crack addicts lurking round Hollywood and Vine. "Y'all have a good night," one shouts, as he returns to his car. Polite, sober zombies, sitting around chatting while they wait for their numbers to reach critical mass are the least of the horrors he will face on tonight's shift.

Around thirty costumed dead turn up in Hollywood in the end. Attendance on a zombie walk varies. King of them all is Pittsburgh, laying claim to 894 stumblers at the Monroeville Mall (location of Romero's classic *Dawn of The Dead*) in October 2006. The average number of attendees is more likely to be in the low tens. Wikipedia defines the zombie walk as just "two or more people dressed as zombies," and sometimes, despite the insistence of MySpace Event invitees that they're bringing "300 friends," no one turns up at all.

Beware Of Flakes

In the ever uncertain world of flesh mobs, it's always a good idea to bring at least one similarly decomposed companion, otherwise you could find yourself looking a complete idiot when all the other attendees find something better to do. It's embarrassing to be the only zombie in a busy crowd of shoppers on a Saturday afternoon, and you might have to deal with a shotgun-wielding mob of the living. Still, the walks go ahead when there are only a few brave souls clutching their bottles of Karo, although their groans might be rather subdued.

Vincent Pogoda was one of "around seven" who staggered up Venice Boardwalk last November. "All great cultural movements start out small and experience exponential growth," he says. "Remember the humble beginnings of the Berlin Love Parade?" How did it feel to be part of such a tiny cadaverous crew? "The cold dead stares of the living as we stumbled down the Boardwalk were...great! Our small numbers made the onlookers confident enough to approach us, and gave us the opportunity to interact personally, thus making it possible to share the joy of being a zombie. We even managed to harvest a few recruits. But we have big plans for the future. Meet me at zombie walk 2012. We will be 7 million strong in 23 nations."

It seems the dead are very determined, and zombie walks, despite some discouraging numbers, continue. Why? Aaron Vanek, horror film-maker and stumbler thinks the walks are popular because "Anybody can be a zombie. Any age, any income level, any race, it's easy to dumb yourself down… " In this fast food nation, the speed of zombification is also attractive. "It's a virus… It's relatively fast acting. Most zombies are instant whereas with vampires, it's a longer process and a conscious entity has to choose to make you one. Werewolves have to wait till the full moon. With a zombie, you're bitten and sooner or later you're going to die and become a zombie yourself. It's that easy."

In an age where identity theft poses a major problem, and people are judged primarily, if not solely, on their looks, voluntary zombification is perhaps an inevitable form of backlash. Even if it is only for a couple of hours. Sean Hoade agrees. "In a zombie walk, you're not *you*—you're *you* after being bitten by a zombie! So it doesn't matter what clothes you wear, how handsome or beautiful you are without gory makeup on, how witty or intelligent you might be—as zombies, everyone is equal!"

Everyone has a zombie alter-ego, a creature for whom nothing matters but forward motion and food. Releasing your inner ghoul is both a cathartic experience and the simplest form of street theatre imaginable, with no lines to remember other than "braaiins!" and "gragh!". Every performer is rewarded with instant celebrity; the stumbling mass stops shoppers in their tracks, and becomes the absolute centre of attention.

"Love Dead ... Hate Living"

Most telling is the reaction of ordinary citizens; smiling, pointing, laughing. It makes their afternoon something special, once they've done the obligatory double take. Those with children hurry past, as there is nothing more likely to inspire awkward questions from Junior ("Mummy! Why has that man's eye fallen out?"). Some want to play too ("Bite me! Make me one of you!") and totally buy into the fake apocalypse scenario. Others just don't get why anyone would do such a thing. "Are they all rich people?" a passing young Latina asks, "rich" being a catch-all term for those who feel they can do what they want, where they want. She seems affronted that the stumblers feel they have the right to do this out in public. "Don't they know Halloween was last year?"

Zombie walks do seem to appeal predominantly to the white middle classes. But is it just a geek thing? Apparently not. Fake death is a great leveller, breaking down even pernicious high school stereotypes. According to Sean Hoades, who observes stumblers on campus zombie walks, "you might have been a sorority girl; you might have been a math geek; you might have been terribly unpopular; you might have been promiscuous; but as zombies, none of these old identities matter one whit. All that matters is preying on the living and making them equal to you as well. This is appealing to almost everyone, but especially to college-age kids."

It's a sign of the times that college age kids avoid active political protest, and instead dress up as the ultimate drop outs. Zombies don't appear to be anti or pro anything. They're not even fighting for their right to party. They represent hopelessness, decay, the breakdown of civilization. They're a one-size-fits-all symbol of the anxieties of our age—homelessness, drug addiction, greed and over-consumption. It's a sad truth that zombies rock our world.

Give Blood! Not Brains!

Yet it's not all about passive-aggressive subversion. One organisation utilises zombie walks for good, using them to promote blood drives or non-perishable food collections. The St Louis-based Zombie Squad (www.zombiehunters.org) uses the concept of zombie invasion to get across important messages about survival and responsibility. Zombies on Main Street might be cute in the broad light of day, but what if they—or terrorists or natural disasters—start to threaten the very fabric of the nation? It's sensible to be prepared.

Kyle Ladd, one of the founders, says Zombie Squad started as a gang of friends who were "big on horror movies. Specifically, zombies and post apocalypse movies like *Mad Max* or *Omega Man*. We didn't have any huge world saving ambitions with ZS at first...[it]...was simply a fun reason for us to get together and watch bad nostalgic movies from our youth."

"We then got a hair up our ass and decided to see if there were other crazies out there like us who also spent an unhealthy amount of time imagining the ultimate worst case scenario and coming up with (and often practising) ideas on how to prepare and survive it. The forum was the start. It drew a lot of attention. Then we decided that maybe we should do something with this large group of people and tried hosting a few charity fund raising movie film festivals."

"It's blown up since then. We have chapters around the country and thousands of members. There almost isn't a month that goes by where there isn't at least one big event going on somewhere. We now host a number of regular charity events, disaster preparation seminars and camping trips throughout the year".

Zombie Squad conducts survival seminars, using tongue in cheek humour (and a "live" zombie) to break down audience's barriers against thinking the unthinkable. Zombies are cool and accessible. Tornadoes, or plagues of killer African bees are not—even if they pose a more immediate threat. These zombies save lives. Post 9/11 and Hurricane Katrina, it's clear that government response to catastrophe might be little more than inadequate. Kyle says "it's irresponsible and dangerous to leave the burden of your survival and well-being on someone else. We've gotten lazy. Our goal is to help promote people to be prepared but we trying to make it fun. That's where the zombie theme comes in. Our motto is if you can be prepared for the walking dead, you can be prepared for just about anything."

That's good to know. Also good to know is that Zombie Squad provide on-the-spot security for zombie walks, keeping a watchful eye on the stumblers. For all their apparent approachability and public usefulness, it's worth remembering that zombies are dangerous brain-sucking scum, out to destroy and assimilate the entire human race. And, surely, a major part of their charm is that they're eminently killable?

Unlike vampires and werewolves, ghouls don't require any specialist kit when it comes to their annihilation. Common everyday objects can be pressed into service. Recent movies have shown us some spectacular zombie elimination techniques, from Simon Pegg's deftly wielded cricket bat in *Shaun of The Dead* to Milla Jovovich's motorbike in *Resident Evil 2*. Games such as *House of The Dead* and *Dead Rising* bring corpse-crunching satisfaction into the comfort of your living room. Everyone has a favourite approach. Kyle Ladd's weapon of choice is "probably a Heckler & Koch HK416 with a titanium crow bar as a back-up." Sean Hoade would agree with Max Brooks (author of the *Zombie Survival Guide*) and go for "a machete. Never needs reloading."

If you're looking for thrills, a way to voice disenchantment, or simply scare people, might it be more appropriate to dress up as a zombie hunter?

Zombie Walk II: Fighting Back

Pedro Miguel Arce plays Pilsbury in Romero's *Land of The Dead* and has seen more than his share of splattered heads in action. He shudders at the very idea of a zombie walk. "It makes me nervous. I don't want to be around this thing and have access to any weapons... Zombies smell bad. They're stenches. They're bad for society—they have nothing to do except walk around rather slowly and feed off good people. They just consume." Another kind of flesh mob altogether brings a glint to his eye, one perhaps timed to coincide with the stumblers, but incorporating nearby rooftops and other vantage points rather than following a street level route. "If that were to happen I want every zombie hunter out there to give me a call and I will gladly lead you."

The zombie walk is a peculiar cultural phenomenon, the nexus of movies, gaming, social networking and urban myth. While it offers huge opportunities for social protest (zombies as anti-war, or anti-poverty marchers, anyone?), most stumblers maintain a distance from what zombies symbolize in society, acknowledging only the 'fun' side of the experience. Up until now, zombie walks have been an underground, unofficial event, generated by fans. But as their profile is raised on both sides of the Atlantic, it's just a matter of time before mass media moves in, sponsoring zombie walks in order to promote a tired movie remake or sequel, or yet another shoot-em-in-the-head game. Then it will be time to add some real edge to the proceedings. Bring on the zombie hunter walk, and let the battle for a nation's *braaainsss* begin.

Alabama zombie expert Sean Hoade fleshes out truths of the undead

By Ben Flanagan

Tuscaloosa resident and author Sean Hoade is an internationally renowned zombie expert. No, seriously. Folks in Canada, Germany and Brazil have all knocked on the doorstep of his temple of undead knowledge, he says.

In summer 2007, Hoade began teaching his class *Zombies! The Living Dead in Literature, Film and Culture* at the <u>University of Alabama</u>, in which, as part of the final exam, students dress themselves as zombies and stalk an unsuspecting campus.

Hoade took a break from the class but will soon, ahem, *revive* it, possibly next spring.

His iTunes U podcast of the same name is getting 90,000 hits per week and is frequently in the top 10 worldwide most downloaded podcasts. He previously recorded the podcasts for the movie website _FilmNerds.com_.

Just in time for Halloween, he talks to us about all things zombies, including what you do if your husband or wife suddenly turns undead.

Ben Flanagan: How about a little word association. When I say, "BRRAAAAAINNNSS!!!!" what first comes to mind?

Sean Hoade: The "Tar Man" from 1985's _Return of the Living Dead_. It was in that movie that the concept of zombies eating brains started. It just caught on, even though killing zombies by brain injury, zombies wanting to eat brains of the living, and "zombiism" being transmitted from zombie to living victim are all mutually exclusive ideas.

BF: As a living zombie, you must know what brains really taste like. Do tell.

SH: Scrambled eggs, in both texture and flavor. Seriously.

BF: What about flesh. That's on the menu as well, isn't it? I've heard it's like chicken.

SH: More like sweet pork. In fact, some Pacific-island cannibals referred to human flesh as "long pig." I've tried the recipe with faux meat. It's quite tasty and harrowing.

BF: It's the zombie apocalypse. What's your weapon and why?

SH: I follow my mentor, *Zombie Survival Guide* author Max Brooks, in this (as in many things): A machete, with sharpening strop. You never have to reload, it works in close quarters, and it doesn't make any undead-attracting noise.

BF: What's the key difference between your average slow-walking zombies and your foaming-at-the-mouth sprinter zombies?

SH: Ah, yes. The fast ones – "Zoombies"—are great with producing the psychological terror of "I'm gonna get you *right now!*" but slow zombies can persevere for much longer, wearing down even the most robust of humans, because their dead muscles don't break down nearly as quickly as those of the fast ones.

BF: If our spouses, kids, best friends or pets go undead on us, what do we do?

SH: Shoot them in the head. Don't wait or feel sorry for them. I would rather be a dead human than a reanimate zombie.

BF: Why don't we ever stop to listen to the zombie? Any chance they spare our brains and just need someone to talk to?

SH: Of course! In fact, while I'm running away, why don't you lean your ear in *really* close to the zombie's mouth and "hear" what it has to "say." You'll soon be repeating it to others!

Top 10 Brain-Eating Zombie Movies

By Ben Flanagan

A great zombie movie must have a strong moral center, according to University of Alabama instructor Sean Hoade.

[Editor's Note: This list was published in 2009. I'd have to find space now for *The Dead* and possibly *Warm Bodies.*]

So what makes a great zombie movie?

We sought out the opinion of international zombie expert and University of Alabama instructor **Sean Hoade**, who says that, first, a great zombie movie must have a tangible moral center.

"In *Dawn of the Dead*, as in most superior zombie flicks, this center lies with the human characters as they try to help one another, whether by saving them or by executing the infected as requested," Hoade said.

In something like famed zombie movie director George A. Romero's *Land of the Dead*, however, the zombies are the moral center. The character "Big Daddy" and his undead crew are trying to carve out a niche for themselves and be left alone by the rampaging humans, Hoade points out and says is a nice twist.

A great zombie movie has memorable characters, according to Hoade, not just interchangeable survivors.

"Think of Shaun and Ed from *Shaun of the Dead*," he said. "They're quirky individuals with goals and flaws. And on some especially memorable occasions, a zombie is an in-duh-vidual. Bub the Zombie from *Day of the Dead* is my all-time favorite!

Finally, Hoade says a great zombie movie must ruthlessly follow its own rules.

"Nothing ruins a zombie flick for me than no rhyme or reason regarding how fast infected humans turn into zombies, what they can and cannot do physically, and whether or not they can 'think' and 'reason,'" he said.

Below are Hoade's top five all-time zombie movies with explanations, starting at the bottom.

5. [REC] (2007) – "This is a masterstroke from Spain: A first-person POV bio-zombie thriller that doesn't miss a paranoid, claustrophobic trick. The walls seem to close in on the characters and the viewer the further things move along. The subtitles make the whole experience even more eerie, like it's a 'found document' along the lines of 'Cloverfield' or 'The Blair Witch Project,' only infinitely scarier. Don't bother with the American remake or the Spanish sequel."

4. **Dawn of the Dead** (2004) – "Really, the only things the remake has in common with the original is survivors trapped in a mall and zombies. Oh, and one other thing: A generational re-imagining of Zombocalypse dread and doom. In exactly the same way that Romero's 'Dawn' showed what zombies could be, Snyder's 'Dawn' revs them up and shows what the 21st century zombie menace could do: In a word, run. The first 10 minutes are

legendary; the rest of the movie is just fun, intensely scary, and consistently intelligent."

3. **Night of the Living Dead (1968)** – "The grandaddy of ghoul flicks, this movie has a special place in my heart because my mother was so freaking scared at a showing of it that she went into labor with me, no joke. But even if George Romero hadn't determined my date of birth, this movie would still have to be high on any list of best zombie movies: Not only did it introduce the concept of the contagious cannibal zombie (there had been contagious ones before, and cannibalistic ones, but to combine them was, obviously, genius), but it is also lean, gloomy, and socially relevant for 1968 and for now, all in equal measures. A brilliant film."

2. **Shaun of the Dead (2004)** – "It isn't just an incredibly funny homage to all things Romero undead; it is also a suspenseful and at times downright scary zombie movie. It works on all levels, every single one. WIN."

1. **Dawn of the Dead (1978)** – "The number one zombie movie ever, the 1978 original is an accomplishment even Romero has never been able to match, try though he has. It's such an absolute

masterpiece of its genre that even its flaws have become part of its legendary appeal. (Why does that biker, in the middle of a zombie feeding frenzy, suddenly sit down to check his blood pressure? Well, duh—how else is he going to get his arm awesomely ripped off in the machine when the zombies grab him and drag him away?) *Dawn* has it all – gruesome zombie menace, real humor and silliness, and biting social commentary when that wasn't expected of a gory horror flick. ('Rosemary's Baby' was very socially relevant, but it was all talk) The pressure of a Zombocalyptic situation is felt in every frame, and the low-budget hacks Romero & Co. had to resort to somehow *enhance* the 'real' feeling of the film, not diminish it. And if you have any remaining doubt about Dawn being the number one zombie movie ever, I have two words for you: THE GONK."

Rounding out Hoade's top 10 are the following zombie movies:

6. *Day of the Dead* (1985)
7. *I Walked With A Zombie* (1943)
8. *Zombi* (aka *Zombi 2*, aka *Zombie Flesh Eaters*) (1979)
9. *White Zombie* (1932)
10. *Zombieland* (2009)

He insists he's not being a purist here when he leaves out *28 Days Later...* and *28 Weeks Later.* He said they come up short because they are *way* overrated, plus they lack the existential and metaphysical dread that is present in the best zombie stories.

Zombies are among us ... and that's OK!

By Mark Hughes Cobb
TUSK Editor

According to Sean Hoade, a University of Alabama English instructor who's taught a popular interim course titled Zombies! *The Living Dead in Literature, Film and Culture*, if zombies seem to be everywhere nowadays, well, that's kind of the point.

They're the villain that multiplies like a virus, an undead, cannibalizing monster swarming by numbers, relentlessness and self-replication, not reliant on intellect, strength, charm or skill.

Zombies may be, after the *Titanic*, the world's biggest metaphor.

Hoade has long been a science-fiction and horror fan, but says he "wouldn't consider myself a supergeek on it."

However, when he watched the 2004 remake of *Dawn of the Dead*, he realized he was more scared of zombies than any ghost, vampire or werewolf.

So he dug into the fear.

"Being an academic, I realized there's a lot of subtext there," Hoade said. In what he laughingly terms "retroactive plagiarism," he found many people had written on topics before he began, about how the zombie in pop culture reflects racial, sexual, religious and family tensions, among others.

Unlike vampires, werewolves, ghosts and witches, which have deep roots in human mythology, zombies are a relative newcomer to the monster scene, although revenants, something like vengeful ghosts, and the "draugr" of medieval Norse mythology, might be related.

William Buehler Seabrook's 1929 book *The Magic Island* introduced the western world to the Vodoun practices of Haiti, in which corpses were said to be reanimated by a sorcerer, and used as common laborers. The 1932 movie *White Zombie* with Bela Lugosi was based loosely on tales from Seabrook's book," as was a stage play of the same name. Occasional movies followed over the decades, but the undisputed progenitor of the modern zombie is director George Romero, who introduced zombies to cannibalism with his landmark *Night of the Living Dead.*

"In 1968, you've got Romero and his friends smoking pot in this old farmhouse, making a movie for $100,000, and they start thinking, 'What is the most attention-grabbing, shocking thing we could have our monsters do?'" Hoade said.

The movie ratings code had just come into being, meaning that, assuming you were willing to bear the R or X, you could get away with, well, murder, of the most gruesome kind.

"So you've got the zombie eating her dead mother, which brings in the incest thing, the cannibalism taboo, matricide … you've got everything," Hoade said.

Romero and company, searching among friends for the best actor, hit on Duane Jones to play the hero, Ben. Jones happened to be black.

"But there's no mention of his race at any time," Hoade said. "In the script, the most competent, reliable, with-it person, wearing a cardigan and Florsheim shoes, just happens to be black. So the zombie movie just happened to become more explicitly about race."

On the ugly side, zombies reflect racist fears: The mob that outdoes the "superior" group by virtue of relentless behavior.

"They've not very fast, they're not very smart, but the thing they can do is replicate very quickly," Hoade said. "It doesn't take any skill, it's just animalistic: They bite somebody.

"What it reflects on, the living become this elite. We can think, we can do all the creative things the zombies can't. But the zombies quickly outnumber us through their sheer, if you want to call it, breeding. It's clearly analogous to what the white supremacists say: 'They're less than us, but they're going to overpower us by their sheer numbers. They will get you by outnumbering you; they will surround you.'"

Zombies contain— in one being—the ideas of *eros* and *thanatos*, the Greek embodiments of lust and death, respectively.

"You literally have the bodies of others erotically charged to you," Hoade said. "We get attracted to people, but the zombie idea perverts this. They will pursue you more than any lover would. They will get to know your flesh much more intimately than any lover could.

"You literally, if you think about it, become one with this other. They physically make you part of them."

That leads to even more disturbing thoughts when a loved one gets bitten.

"If you have someone who is literally your lover before she's turned into a zombie, she's still her, but she's not her. When you become a lover with someone, you basically give them access to your body. Do you rescind that when they become a zombie? I think you probably should," Hoade said, laughing.

But he notes that's how many zombie horrors work: By showing survivors reacting to loved ones who have turned on them.

"She's not your mother anymore, but she still looks and feels the same, mostly, to you," Hoade said. "That's the uncanny. That's why Freud says it's such a sometimes devastating experience to go back to your hometown when you've been away for many years.

"Zombies fit into that wish we sometimes have, that a dead loved one could return. OK, they're not dead anymore... but they're worse."

Zombie movies help audiences reflect on ideas about civilization collapsing in a way that's strangely relatable, and still enjoyable.

"Like in *Dawn of the Dead*, you've got a small group of survivors fighting for their lives in a shopping mall," Hoade said, alluding to yet another zombie metaphor, eating human flesh translates to rampant human consumerism. "That's fun. But compare that to a movie like *The Day After*, about nuclear war. That's not fun! That could really happen.

"So it's a safe way to think about the end of the world, and also a safe way to think about death, in its natural state [of mortification]. There's a curiosity about that throughout most of human history, but our culture has sort of kept that hidden away, which I'm fine with," Hoade said, laughing.

Before the zombies stopped lumbering and started running—as did the so-called "zoombies" of the 2004 *Dawn of the Dead* remake—the key to zombie success was their simplicity. As Max Brooks wrote in his hit 2003 book, *The Zombie Survival Guide*, zombies don't stop to relieve themselves, sleep or eat.

"But you are their dinner," Hoade said, "and you *do* have to stop. You have your human limitations."

Zombies are limited, too, of course, which explains why they're just now reaching literature, after decades of success in movies (including more whimsical adaptations of recent years, such as 2004's *Shaun of the Dead* and Troma Films' 2008 *Poultrygeist: Night of the Chicken Dead*, starring Tuscaloosa-born actor Kate Graham) videogames (the Resident Evil and Doom series, among others) and comics.

"The only other fictional zombie novel that I know of is *World War Z*, by Max Brooks," said Seth Grahame-Smith, author of the newly released collaboration with Jane Austen, *Pride and Prejudice and Zombies*. "Mine is without a doubt the first foray for zombies into classical literature.

"One of the problems is, and I guess Mary Shelley (author of *Frankenstein: The Modern Prometheus*) found a way to get around this, zombies don't talk. And because they don't talk, they're this big monolithic problem that stumbles across the countryside until somebody shoots enough of them in the brain.

"You can't reason with them, you can't write dialogue for them. Basically all you can do is chop their heads off or run away from them."

In films, you can get away with such lack of acumen by focusing on the visual splendor of a dripping corpse chowing on a meaty thigh.

And of course, the metaphors.

"Romero used them to symbolize everything from Vietnam to consumerism," Grahame-Smith said. "They've always been used to comment on the social ills of the day, but they don't DO much. They're really single-minded, but they're not doing it out of hate, not doing it out of spite. This is a virus."

Which leads to yet another zombie metaphor, for the potential fallout of ugly warfare.

But is the zombie, as one blogger suggested, the new vampire?

"I think vampires are still the new vampires," Grahame-Smith said. "There's going to be three more 'Twilight' movies in the next years."

Hoade believes the current spate of zombie novelty literature—*Pride and Prejudice and Zombies*, Brooks' survival guide—will lead to new, more serious fiction on zombies, focusing, as the most zombie pop does, on the survivors and not the monsters themselves.

"It could be a serious examination of what it would mean to live in a world of zombies," he said. "And *World War Z* was an excellent example of this; it took it really seriously. Humans had a war with zombies, and we almost lost, but there are still zombies. What would life be like knowing there's always that threat?"

Like, say—rolling metaphor alert—living in a world with the sword of terrorism hanging over your heads?

Our current financial troubles, seemingly bleak and endless, could mean happy days for zombies and other monsters, Hoade said.

"That's the time when escapist literature really takes off," he said. "When we have a war, technology benefits. When we have financial depressions, artistic creativity seems to take off.

"Now that the zombie infestation has spread to public-domain novels, next thing you're going to have movies based on those novels. *City Lights* with zombies? *Rachel Getting Buried?*" he said, laughing. "It's going to be fun getting there, whatever it is."

The European

"The Zombie Is The New Vampire"

The European wrote about zombies and me. In German. The original version is below, but first, here's a handy and extremely amusing automated translation! Thanks, Google!

The undead have a sensational rise behind and are now the archetypal monsters of our time. Sean Hoade, an expert on the zombie in the literature at the University of Alabama, explains why.

The European: Mister Hoade, since the 60s we know the zombie out of the movies, but

really arrived in the literature it is not until much later. Why is that?

The zombie was always a very critical issue as novel. He is so dull in the head, that he hardly passes as a subject, but rather as an object. In the movie, where the monster does not need inner life, that's okay. But in literature? Since figures must have the ability for self-reflection, they must ponder and can perform internal transformations. Vampires, werewolves and ghosts are in the best position to. Zombies do not, which makes them unsuitable as characters, and yet who uses them in books, was until recently just always the same, apocalyptic tale of the people on the edge of her doom tell.

The European: Today the zombies shuffle but quite successfully through the book market, so it must have obviously changed something. What exactly?

It actually began 10 to 15 years ago, as more and more short stories started to describe the inner workings of such people who were bitten by zombies and were on the verge of becoming undead themselves. So there was finally a reflection, the material, the literature needs to breathe. Thus began the real zombie literature, and I mean that fewer books and more trash magazines and dime novels, but still.

The European: How the undead then came from the dime novel to the literature?

The truly groundbreaking next step came with ironic, winking works such as Max Brooks' Zombie Survival Guide. " Based on an imaginative zombie epidemic, he explains to the reader how best to respond to the life-threatening situation. By the reader like an insider in the fictional location, but it reflects the reality unconsciously. Another literary effect also have books like "Pride and Prejudice and Zombies" – humor, a mixture of Jane Austen and a zombie tale. Just by the context of the existing classic novel is alienated, we are forced to reflect on the original new: The world in Jane Austen's original, it is clear to us when reading, is not a bit less than the fictional world of the recently published zombie parody. This makes it clear that zombie novels have as their literary legitimacy as the novels of Jane Austen and Charles Dickens. Because they accomplish what needs to achieve literature: they help us cope with the reality.

The European: Meanwhile, the zombie is considered archetypal monsters of our time, as the epitome of terror in the postmodern era. As he comes to this honor?

Well, actually, the zombie is, if you will, the new vampire, the counterpart of blood suckers or werewolves before. To their heyday in the literature, there was really foreign cultures, wildlife, dense forests. They were also a metaphor for the dangers that threaten us from these areas. What we have instead today, at least in the so-called civilized world are endless crowds. Of them today comes from the real threat. My fear is not more that I get lost in the woods, but that someone shoots me or my children out of the blue. And as the zombie can also look like the murderer of ordinary man on the street, like my neighbor, as anyone's.

The European: Horror Director George Romero used the figure of the zombie hand as a metaphor for the mindless, insatiable consumers. Are there other interpretations?

Romero's interpretation is the most obvious, in fact. Zombies running around mindlessly for all eternity in search of eating in a circle, basically what they were doing as consumers before their demise. This of course comes directly from Dante's "Inferno", where the damned are cursed to see her old life with all faults for all eternity in hell. Another metaphor would be to look at the healthy people as the social elite, the zombies, however, than the lower layer, which is perceived as a threat from above: you follow their animal instincts, breed like crazy and are slowly but surely the majority.

The European: What exactly does the zombie really so horrible?

We orient ourselves to Sigmund Freud's distinction between "secret" and "scary". The uncanny, he says, the secret is very, very similar. The two are almost identical, just a tiny bit wrong with the uncanny. This is also true for the zombie: He may look just like your mother, he may even put in their body, but boy: This is not your mother. This is much, much scarier than a man who turns into a wolf or a bat. From vampires or werewolves can knit romantic hero. From zombies? No chance. This is something else: In the West we like to trivialize death, our dead be made up, dressed up and embedded in silk cushions. With the zombies is a part of the horrible, dirty reality of death to the surface. It's always terrible.

And below is the original! Probably I come off as pretty awesome, but they could be calling me "sad butt boy" the whole time and I'd never know it.

„Der Zombie ist der neue Vampir"

Die Untoten haben einen sensationellen Aufstieg hinter sich und sind heute das archetypische Monster unserer Zeit. Sean

Hoade, Experte für den Zombie in der Literatur an der University of Alabama, erklärt warum.

The European: Mister Hoade, schon seit den 60ern kennen wir den Zombie aus dem Kino, so richtig in der Literatur angekommen ist er aber erst wesentlich später. Woran liegt das?

Der Zombie hatte als Romanfigur immer ein ganz entscheidendes Problem. Er ist so stumpf im Kopf, dass er kaum mehr als Subjekt durchgeht, sondern eher als Objekt. Im Film, wo das Monster kein Innenleben braucht, ist das okay. Aber in der Literatur? Da müssen Figuren die Fähigkeit zur Selbstreflexion haben, sie müssen grübeln und innere Wandlungen vollziehen können. Vampire, Werwölfe und Gespenster sind dazu bestens in der Lage. Zombies nicht, das macht sie als Figuren untauglich, und wer sie trotzdem in Büchern verwendet, konnte bis vor einiger Zeit nur immer dieselbe, apokalyptische Geschichte von den Menschen am Rande ihres Untergangs erzählen.

The European: Heute schlurfen die Zombies aber ganz erfolgreich durch den Buchmarkt,

also muss sich offensichtlich etwas verändert haben. Was genau?

Es begann eigentlich vor 10 bis 15 Jahren, als immer mehr Kurzgeschichten begannen, die inneren Prozesse solcher Menschen zu beschreiben, die von Zombies gebissen wurden und kurz davor standen, selbst ein Untoter zu werden. Da gab es also endlich eine Reflexion, den Stoff, den Literatur zum Atmen braucht. Damit begann die echte Zombie-Literatur, wobei ich damit weniger Bücher meine und mehr Trash-Magazine und Groschenromane, aber immerhin.

The European: Wie kamen die Untoten dann vom Groschenroman in die Literatur?

Der wirklich bahnbrechende nächste Schritt kam erst mit ironischen, augenzwinkernden Werken wie Max Brooks "Zombie Survival Guide". Auf der Basis einer imaginativen Zombie-Epidemie erklärt er dem Leser, wie er am besten auf die lebensbedrohliche Situation reagiert. Indem der Leser sich in die fiktive Lage hineinversetzt, reflektiert er aber unbewusst auch die Wirklichkeit. Einen anderen, ebenfalls literarischen Effekt haben Bücher wie "Pride and Prejudice and Zombies" – eine humoreske Mischung aus Jane Austen und einer Zombie-Fabel. Gerade indem der Kontext des schon vorhandenen Romanklassikers verfremdet wird, werden wir gezwungen, das Original neu zu reflektieren: Die Welt in Jane Austens Vorlage, wird uns beim Lesen klar, ist kein bisschen weniger fiktiv als die Welt der jetzt erschienenen Zombie-Parodie. Damit wird deutlich, dass Zombie-Romane genauso ihre literarische Legitimation haben wie die Romane von Jane Austen oder Charles Dickens. Denn sie erreichen, was Literatur erreichen muss: Sie helfen uns bei der Wirklichkeitsbewältigung.

The European: Mittlerweile gilt der Zombie als archetypisches Monster unserer Zeit, als Inbegriff des Schrecklichen in der Postmoderne. Wie kommt er zu dieser Ehre?

Nun, tatsächlich, der Zombie ist, wenn man so will, der neue Vampir, das Gegenstück zu Blutsaugern oder Werwölfen früher. Zu deren Blütezeit in der Literatur gab es noch wirklich fremde Kulturen, Wildnis, dichte Waldflächen. Sie waren auch eine Metapher für die Gefahren, die uns aus diesen Bereichen drohen. Was wir stattdessen heute haben, zumindest in der sogenannten zivilisierten Welt, sind endlose Menschenmengen. Von ihnen geht heute die wirkliche Bedrohung aus. Meine Angst ist doch nicht mehr, dass ich mich im Wald verlaufe, sondern dass irgendjemand mich oder meine Kinder aus dem Blauen heraus erschießt. Und wie der Zombie kann auch der Mörder aussehen wie der ganz normale Mann auf der Straße, wie mein Nachbar, wie jedermann.

The European: Horrorfilmregisseur George Romero benutzte die Figur des Zombies dagegen als Metapher für den geistlosen, unersättlichen Konsumenten. Gibt es noch andere Deutungen?

Romeros Deutung ist in der Tat die Offensichtlichste. Zombies, die stumpfsinnig in alle Ewigkeit auf der Suche nach Fressen im Kreis herumlaufen, im Grunde das, was sie als Konsumenten schon vor ihrem Ableben taten. Das stammt natürlich direkt aus Dantes "Inferno", wo die Verdammten dazu verflucht werden, ihr altes Leben mit allen Fehlern bis in alle Ewigkeit in der Hölle zu erleben. Eine andere Metapher wäre, die gesunden Menschen als die gesellschaftliche Elite zu betrachten, die

Zombies hingegen als die Unterschicht, die von oben als Bedrohung wahrgenommen wird: Sie folgen ihren tierischen Instinkten, vermehren sich wie verrückt und werden langsam aber sicher zur Mehrheit.

The European: Was genau macht den Zombie eigentlich so grauenhaft?

Orientieren wir uns an Sigmund Freuds Unterscheidung von "heimlich" und "unheimlich". Das Unheimliche, sagt er, ist dem Heimlichen sehr, sehr ähnlich. Fast sind die beiden identisch, nur ein ganz kleines bisschen stimmt nicht mit dem Unheimlichen. Das gilt auch für den Zombie: Er sieht vielleicht genauso aus wie deine Mutter, möglicherweise steckt er sogar in ihrem Körper, aber Junge: Das ist nicht deine Mutter. Das ist viel, viel unheimlicher als ein Mann, der sich in einen Wolf oder eine Fledermaus verwandelt. Aus Vampiren oder Werwölfen kann man romantische Helden stricken. Aus Zombies? Keine Chance. Dazu kommt noch etwas: Im Westen verniedlichen wir den Tod gerne: Unsere Verstorbenen werden geschminkt, kostümiert und in Seidenkissen gebettet. Mit den Zombies kommt ein Teil der schrecklichen, schmutzigen Wirklichkeit des Todes an die Oberfläche. Das ist immer grauenhaf.

FILMNERDS

Since 2008, *FilmNerds.com* has been providing our own unique, decidedly nerdy take on film, with in-depth looks at both classic and contemporary films.

Check out some of the cimemafantastical features you'll find at *FilmNerds.com!*

FilmNerds Unlimited Podcast
High-caliber movie discussions with high-quality movie connoisseurs

The Great Scenes
A detailed look at some of the greatest individual scenes in the history of cinema.

Back to the Movies
Journey back to the 1980s to see what we were watching and how it holds up today.

Find your seat, get your popcorn ready, and visit *FilmNerds.com!*

About the Authors

SEAN HOADE scribbles his mad tomes in the wilds of Las Vegas, Nevada, which provides plenty of apocalyptic inspiration. He taught at the University of Alabama for almost 10 years, including groundbreaking for-credit classes on zombies, superheroes, and the Apocalypse, all of which attracted international attention. His seven-part lecture series on zombies in film, literature, and culture receives 90,000 downloads each year from iTunes U.

Sean's zombies-in-Las-Vegas novel, *Reviva Las Vegas!* is available in ebook formats and in delicious paperback. He lectures on fiction, contributes to panels, and gives readings at Conventions all over the country, and welcomes you to visit him at **SeanHoade.com** and drop him an email at **sean@seanhoade.com**.

MATT SCALICI is a lifelong enthusiast of many frivolous pursuits, one of which is film. He's the owner/editor of **FilmNerds.com**, where he writes and podcasts about movies. When he's not watching movies, Matt is the managing producer of sports for **AL.com**, the largest news organization in the state of Alabama. Matt lives in Birmingham, AL with his wife, Francesca, and two children, Naomi and Ennio.